D1488767

BACKYARDS, BOW TIES, & BEAUTY QUEENS

By BILL THOMPSON

Published by Our State, Mann Media Inc.
Greensboro, North Carolina

Library of Congress Cataloging-in-Publication Data

Thompson, Bill, 1943 Sept. 18-
Backyards, Bow Ties, & Beauty Queens / Bill Thompson.
    p. cm.
ISBN 978-0-9779681-4-5 (pbk. : alk. paper)
1. North Carolina--Social life and customs--Anecdotes. 2.
Country life--North Carolina--Anecdotes. 3. City and town life--
North Carolina--Anecdotes. 4. North Carolina--Biography--
Anecdotes. 5. Thompson, Bill, 1943, Sept. 18- --Anecdotes. I. Title.
II. Title: Backyards, Bow Ties, & Beauty Queens.
F254.6.T475 2008
975.6--dc22
                                                    2008021370

For my grandchildren —
Drew, Mia, Caroline, Currie, and Paige

TABLE OF CONTENTS

ACKNOWLEDGEMENTS

On this page, I'm supposed to acknowledge all the folks who have helped me bring all this together. Since this is a collection of essays, and, by definition, essays are personal opinions and stories directly connected to the writer, that means everybody with whom I have ever come in contact has a part in this.

Literally hundreds of people have told me stories I've used in compiling and painting this picture. I don't remember all their names; I remember most of their faces, but I can't forget how much their involvement means to me. This book is truly an assimilation of all I have been a part of, and without the participation of each person, I could not have written it.

There are certainly those patient, encouraging souls who have seen fit to give me another opportunity to do something I enjoy. The people at *Our State* magazine are very special people who allow me a great amount of freedom in what I choose to write about. In nearly a decade of sending in columns and articles for the magazine and two previous books, they have seldom rejected anything. I certainly don't object when they correct my grammar, clarify my sentence structure, or suggest that something needs to be changed to make more sense. Vicky Jarrett is the quintessential "Steel Magnolia," a smart, busy lady with definite opinions but in her charming way makes you feel that your opinions are just as important. And Cathy Kelly, Bernie Mann, and Amy Jo Wood have always been there to encourage me and find a way to make my books sell. Thank you all.

To my family, thanks for your patience and encouragement. And to my creditors, thanks for hanging in there, guys. Your name is back in the hat.

PREFACE

In putting this book together, I wanted to paint a picture of North Carolina in all its diversity, both physical and cultural. What you're holding in your hands is the most eclectic mural I could have imagined — everything from trusting chickens, to playing banjos and listening to opera, to mule deaths and skinny-dipping in the creek. In and around all that are my reflections about who we are as North Carolinians and how we can preserve and conserve all we have.

For nearly 40 years, I have been fortunate enough to travel the length and breadth of this state talking to people, sharing in celebrations, and observing changes. One of the elements I found to be most common among North Carolinians is a sense of humor, along with an inclination — even a compulsion — to tell stories. Almost every time I speak to a group, someone will come up after the event and want to tell me a story. I love to listen because those stories reveal so much about the storyteller, too. Then that person becomes a part of me.

I really became aware of the scope of my written mural when I was trying to think of a title for the book. This is my third book about North Carolina, a kind of sequel to *Sweet Tea, Fried Chicken, & Lazy Dogs*, my first book. For this book, even my ideas for a title were diverse: Pictures Painted With a Tarheel Mind; Of Peanuts, Lawn Parties, Politics and Why I love It All; Barbecue, Beauty Pageants, and the Folks Next Door; Wastrels, Saints, and Their Mules: A Written Picture of North Carolina Life; Whatever Happened to That Time You Forgot; High Tea With Barbecue and Hushpuppies; Y'all Ain't Gonna Believe What Happened; and Stories from the General Store, Family Reunions, and Some I Just Made Up. It's hard enough to capture the heart and soul of a place and people without putting it all in a pithy, concise title.

During the writing of this book, I became very much aware of how everything in the state has changed and continues to change. Change is inevitable, but I hope that by writing about those elements of our Carolina life that have ceased to be or have changed to something else entirely I can preserve that sense of being a part of a special time and place that is unique to us North Carolinians. Someone asked me once why I write so much about the past. I told them that the future is unknown, and the present is so fleeting that the past is the only thing certain. And nostalgia can edit the past to be what we want it to be.

What I hope you get from this book is just simple enjoyment. It has been fun to write. Most of the stories are humorous — I hope they bring a smile or a chuckle. Feel free to laugh out loud. Some stories might make you stop and think a little about life in general. And I hope many will cause you to reflect a little bit on how fortunate we are to live in such a wonderful place as North Carolina.

I hope you enjoy it.

Bill Thompson
April 1, 2008

Backyards, Bow Ties, & Beauty Queens

backyard philosopher

Why I Wear a Bow Tie

Several years ago I took to wearing bow ties. The original reason had to do with the fact that I was more frustrated with paying cleaning bills for my long ties than I was concerned about any fashion statement I might make. If I were real honest, I'd have to say that the frequency of my dropping food on my ties increased as my stomach pushed my tie in the way of errant food.

That waist expansion did not lend itself to my ability to look good in any kind of attire anyway. So I thought I might as well adopt a more practical approach to my neckwear.

But the transition was not as simple as I thought it would be. I could not bring myself to wear one of those clip-on ties. If I was really going to adopt this new mode of dress, I wanted to do it the right way. That meant I had to learn how to tie a bow tie.

So while I was in Charlotte I went to a specialty tie store and looked at a bunch of bow ties and asked the sales lady to show me how to tie one. She put the tie around her neck and easily created the perfect bow. My attempt resulted in a knot of indescribable ugliness.

Then she suggested that she stand behind me and tie it on me to help me learn the technique. She was very polite about it, so I agreed. I don't know if anybody was walking by as the activity was taking place, but I feel sure that an observer would have been more than amused to see this tall, bulky body of mine trying to squat down far enough for this little girl to reach around me and tie that tie. It looked like she was going to jump on my back for a ride and use the tie for the reins. I finally told her I'd just buy the tie and take it home and figure out how to tie it myself.

I did learn how to tie a bow tie, although I still don't make the neatest bow. But I've found that a lot of other gentlemen who wear bow ties aren't much better at it than me. In fact, I read in a magazine that how a man ties a bow tie is a statement of his individuality. After looking at my handiwork, I believe I can say that I am pretty much an individual.

Naturally, after I started wearing a bow tie on a regular basis, I began to notice other people who wore them. I found them everywhere.

I think a lot of doctors wear bow ties because they stay out of the way during the examination of a patient. I'm sure that patients appreciate this concern since they probably don't like to have the doctor hold the tie back with one hand as he uses the other hand to determine if gall bladder surgery is needed.

I noticed in particular that many pediatricians wear bow ties. The obvious reason there, of course, is that a baby patient is less likely to grab hold of a bow tie and choke the doctor during the examination. A long tie hanging down in front of a baby is too much of a temptation.

I also noticed a lot of college professors and lawyers wearing them. In both cases, I think it's a matter of tradition. When I think back to the professors I had in college, I'm sure that many of them wore bow ties because a precedent had been set by their professors. The same thing applies to lawyers as much as you can make any kind of general statement about why lawyers do anything.

I guess the greatest affirmation of my sartorial choice in regard to my neckwear is related to my admiration for one of my favorite literary characters, who happens to be a lawyer. Atticus Finch, the heroic lawyer and father in *To Kill a Mockingbird*, wore a bow tie. I can't think of a better character to emulate.

Why I Haven't Lost My Marbles

I am probably the only person in the world who doesn't know what a Pokemon is. I don't even know if that's the correct way to spell it. Whatever it is, it's not the first nor, doubtless, the last such invention to take over the minds and money of today's children. Remember the hula-hoop? Cabbage Patch dolls? Matchbox cars?

I have mentioned at other times the propensity for children to play with boxes that expensive toys come in. I still believe that a child's creative imagination can come up with more interesting toys than anything we adults can contrive.

For instance, I believe that a child invented marbles. No adult could come up with something so simple: little glass balls with all the colorful hues that could catch the eye of a child. A game of marbles requires no electricity (batteries or otherwise), and no assembly is required. The rules of the game aren't written in three languages on the back of the box it came in. Marbles don't always even come in a box!

The main attraction to marbles is not the game itself. Certainly it is a great game, a game of skill and strategy. But the main attraction for me is the marbles themselves. There's something sensual about the smooth feel of the marbles — something about that spherical shape that challenges you. You can't stack marbles without some foreign constraint; their smoothness makes them elusive. You can't push them together. Their hardness makes them resilient. You can force them against each other, but it's almost impossible to break one marble with another — they just bounce off.

Each marble is unique. I'm sure that there may be some marble somewhere that's an exact duplicate of another, but if you look at it long enough, a marble's appearance will change right before your eyes. The shade of a color will darken or brighten as the sun's rays strike it. Once you find one that seems to be a genuine one-of-a-kind, that's a keeper. Its value is far above rubies. You don't even put it in the ring for fear it may be taken.

When I was a boy, marbles used to come either in a great big jar or in small bags. They were relatively inexpensive. If you were lucky or looked hard enough, you might run up on a marble that was bigger than the others. That was the shooter. Sometimes, depending on the neighborhood, some guy would come up with a "steelie": a ball bearing gouged out of a piece of metal found down at the local garage. In some neighborhoods, a steelie was illegal — the legality being determined by majority vote of the players. Of course, if the guy who owned the steelie happened to be much bigger than any other player, the rule could be waived.

Serious marble players carried their marbles in a small sack; the rest of us kept them in our pocket. That's why marbles had such a unique smell. I know you may wonder who smelled marbles. Well, I did. If you carried around all those marbles in your pocket for a while, they would take on the smell of that pocket. Depending on what else you had in your pocket, the smell could be of apples or oranges or motor oil or the good clean smell of dirt. The smell made them yours.

Pokemon and Nintendo will never replace marbles. Some time, somewhere, a shiny, colorful sphere will catch the eye of an imaginative child — yet again.

In the Spring a Young Man Turns

It seems like spring is the shortest season of the year. It starts with temperatures that slip from the low 40s in the day to a night frost that kills everybody's tomato plants. Sometimes we have moved frost-threatened flowers in and out of the house so often the bottom of the pots get worn out. Then before you know it, the weather can also be so warm that a leisurely stroll brings out the perspiration; the lakes and rivers fill with boaters and pale sunbathers, who are already turning pink.

Each year I can't help but notice how the quick transition of the season coincides with school graduations, both college and high school. Like the change within the season, there doesn't seem to be a very long transition period now for the graduates, either. College graduates, particularly, will immediately have to change their everyday attire from baggy pants and sweatshirts to suits and ties.

The biggest adaptation, however, will have more to do with how they live than how they dress. Accepting responsibility for their everyday existence will be a challenge for some who have relied on their parents for rent money, automobile insurance, electricity bills, phone bills, and all the other costs of living. For some, it will be a shock. For others it will just be one more step toward maturity. In either case, like the changing season, there's not much time to adjust.

It wasn't too long ago that I had a son graduating from college one spring. Fortunately for him, this life-passage was just another step toward adulthood. It took him awhile to accept the inevitability of maturation, but he has done so and is moving on. Like most fathers, I felt compelled to pass on a portion of my accumulated wisdom to him at the time. So, here it is:

- Never forget who you are. Be proud of your heritage, but don't be "prideful." We're the only ones who think that all our geese are swans.

- Go to church every Sunday. Beyond all the benefits you will receive from attendance, it's something you are supposed to do as member of this family and the family of God.

- Get only one credit card. One is a necessity; two is a temptation. More than two are a burden.

- If you work for a man, give him a full day's work. He is paying you for a full day's work; if you give him less, you are stealing from him.

- Have confidence in your abilities, but never be afraid to learn from other people. Everybody makes mistakes. Learn from yours and everybody else's as well.

- Read at least one book a month. Never let television, movies, or the Internet replace books.

- Write letters. It's easier to use the telephone or email, but writing a letter is more personal. You can't see teardrops on email. Your handwriting is an extension of your mind and heart — share it.

- Set aside some time just for yourself. Never be so busy that you don't have time to stop and think about the real world around you.

- Take in every drop of life. Don't sip it; drink it down in great gulps. There's so much to do and see, so many people to meet and know, so many experiences to be a part of that you have to grasp every opportunity when it presents itself — then savor it later.

I'm sure my son won't take all that advice, but maybe he'll learn it for himself during the lifelong maturation process.

Late Night Musings

Over the past 40 years or so, I've spent a lot of time traveling throughout the South at night alone in an automobile. Usually it was a return trip from some evening speaking engagement. If I had nothing scheduled in that area for the next morning (and because I'm too cheap to pay for a hotel room), I'd make my way back home.

An offshoot of that lonely excursion is a weird (for lack of a better word) reflection on the state of the world, my neighbors, and life in general. Many years ago, I would try to remember those thoughts the next day to no avail. Later, I got a little tape recorder to take with me and spoke my musings into the machine. Just recently I found that old tape recorder. The batteries were dead, and the little tiny tape was so scratchy I could hardly understand what I'd said, even after I put new batteries in the machine. But I listened to it all as best I could and realized some of what I'd said was pertinent only at the time I said it. In other cases, I found that I made some observations that might hold true even today. Admittedly, some — maybe most — of them are trivial, but I wrote them down this time.

1. Nobody will ever put out a sign that reads "NICE DOG."
2. I believe that the average woman talks 50 percent more than the average man listens. I also believe that no woman thinks she's average.

3. There's no such thing as "a simple little job around the house." Every job becomes complex because I either don't have the right tools or someone comes along who will tell me a better way to get the job done.
4. Eventually, everything we do or eat will kill us.
5. I believe that smoking is the leading cause of statistics. Never in the history of mankind has anything been so studied by so many with so little objectivity.
6. You should never eat prunes when you're hungry.
7. The greatest investment in the world today is computer paper. (I recorded this thought at a time before everything was recorded on CDs, USB, or any of the other modern computer devices that has replaced paper.)
8. I believe that it's logical to assume that a fat person uses more soap that a thin person. In all honesty, I have no empirical evidence to substantiate this statement, and the possibility of gathering any is extremely unlikely given the nature of the study.
9. There's no such thing as half a hole.
10. You can't convince a stoplight that you are in a hurry. In fact, I don't think we should argue with inanimate objects. Not only is it a waste of time, but we will lose the argument.
11. Nobody really cares about apathy.
12. There's more to making love that just the exercise. The older I get the more convinced I become.
13. The man that invented the eraser had a lot of insight into human nature. However, his genius would have been wasted had not someone invented the graphite pencil.
14. Most people use credit cards because they don't have money in the bank to cover the purchase.
15. The United States Constitution has to be the greatest document ever written. How else could this country have survived all the politicians who have tried to manipulate it?

16. In this imperfect world, there is not a solution to every problem, but there is a problem for every solution.

17. The government can never be run like a business because the boss (or bosses) can be fired by the employees.

18. I am convinced that the best definition of infinity is one lawyer waiting for another. This observation is based on my experience of dealing with lawyers everyday.

19. If other people's problems ceased to exist, most of us wouldn't have anything to talk about.

20. I've got to quit taking long trips at night by myself.

A Philosophical Moment in Time

Some events may be so wonderful that we never want to lose that feeling of elation. That feeling has been the theme of poems, songs, and stories for years. Englebert Humperdink the Second (not the German composer of the opera *Hansel and Gretel*) recorded a song entitled "One Moment in Time" that was very popular back in the 1970s. H.G. Wells wrote about traveling back in time in *The Time Machine*. Just think what would actually happen if we froze time — if time stood still.

Is there any single event in your life that you would choose to relive at the exclusion of everything else?

How about the first time you fell in love? Sociologists say most of us experience that first real love when we are teenagers. Of course, so much is changing in our lives at that time that even that great emotional experience just seems to fall in line with all the other life-changing elements, including physical and intellectual development.

What about a religious experience? Did some epiphany occur that enlightened your life and made you aware of some new meaning to your life that never occurred before?

And how about when your first child was born? How wonderful it was to see and feel and touch that small life that was a part of you and someone you loved very much. Can that feeling be surpassed?

All of those things are wonderful, happy experiences, but life is not all happy experiences. There are hundreds of other life experiences that mold our lives. Some of them sad. Each experience changes us in some way. Would we want to stop time when something good, really good, happens to the exclusion of anything else happening in our lives?

No, probably not. You can't have a rainbow without some rain, and you can't have any more great experiences if we never go on after that one ecstatic moment, regardless of how wonderful it may have been.

Knowing our lives could be extinguished in the blink of an eye, we would be foolish not to drink in everyday in big gulps and little sips that savor the moment. There's too much to see and do — and too many people to meet — to lock in one moment in time.

A fellow named Don Harold once wrote (borrowing from Nadine Stair), "If I had my life to live over, I would start barefoot earlier in the spring and stay that way later in the fall. I would play hooky more. I would have more dogs. I would keep later hours. I'd have more sweethearts. I would fish more. I would go to more dances. I would ride more merry-go-rounds. I would pick more daises."

You can't do any of that unless you move on.

My Stand on the Tobacco Question

This era of political correctness is fraught with pitfalls for those who choose to tread the halls of government. It's never been easy to place oneself in a position of influence without offending those whom we wish to influence. Navigating that uneasy path is a sign of a statesman. That's certainly been the case as our congressional representatives have struggled with the tobacco question. Of course, the tobacco buyout has lessened the debate somewhat, but the controversy still remains even if somewhat dormant.

One such man comes to mind as I listen to the political leaders of our tobacco-producing state struggle to continue to represent their constituents while maintaining at least a semblance of power and influence in a time when so many think of tobacco as the scourge of mankind.

The gentleman I am reminded of did not come from a tobacco state. He was an attorney and a distinguished member of the legislature in Mississippi at a time when that state was legally "dry." With the true eloquence so common to Southern statesmen, N.S. Sweat Jr. answered the question of his position regarding liquor with such equanimity that his response stands as a guide to all who face a similar challenge.

With Sweat's response to the liquor question as my guide, I propose an answer to the question of whether tobacco is, indeed, the "wicked weed" or a maligned element of Carolina pride:

If, when you say "tobacco," you mean that noxious vegetation whose cultivation involves the emission of toxic chemicals into the very air we breath; if you mean the plant whose burning leaves create a smoke that permeates the lungs of young and old alike eating away at the very tissue of that organ of life, a smoke that causes a stench in the clothes we wear, the furniture on which we sit, and the very breath we breathe; if you mean that agricultural endeavor whose harvest has caused young men to toil in the sun until they collapse from heat exhaustion; if you mean that dried weed whose dust clogs the nostrils and fills the very pores of the skin until it's black as a sinner's heart, then I am against it.

But if, by "tobacco," you mean that product of the Carolina soil that's been the source of livelihood for thousands of families for generations; that's provided the funds that have sent the offspring of poor tenant farmers to college; that's built churches where the loving spirit of The Creator is made known to all who enter its doors; that's kept many an able-bodied man off the welfare roles and filled the coffers of every clothier, grocer, and merchant in the small towns across this state; if you mean that commodity from which the sale thereof produced the taxes that paved the roads that now traverse the length and breath of this great state and built the schools that have educated and continue to educate the leaders of our communities; if you mean that golden leaf whose heady aroma emitted from the curing barn wafts its way through the summer night weaving its spell like the perfume of a beautiful woman; if you mean that product that's given solace and comfort to those who have come to the end of day in which they have struggled mightily to make a living from the land or who have finally found respite from the heat and monotony of the mill; if you mean that smoke created in the bowl of a pipe as men sit together in commonality and devise solutions to the social ills that beset us; if you mean that cigar offered as congratulations at the birth of a child or proffered as a reward for achievement; if you mean that crop whose history is irretrievably tied to the history and development of this state, the South, and this country, then, my friend, I am for it.

That's my stand, and I'm sticking to it.

Not Just A Tree

Many years ago, I worked in the woodlands division of a paper company. My job as public relations director was to present a positive image of the company and the industry to the public. My employment came about at the same time there was an increasing interest in the environment. Therefore, much of my activity involved trying to convince the public that the paper company was a good steward of the vast woodlands they managed.

One of the most active conservation groups I encountered when I worked for the paper company was the Sierra Club. They seemed to think that every time a tree was cut the company should suffer guilt and be punished for its "uncaring" action. I disagreed then, and I disagree now, but I do think that we should all be more aware of the gifts that trees bring to our daily lives.

When I was a little boy, there was a small cedar tree in the corner of the churchyard next to my house. My sister and I used to take turns pulling each other in a little red wagon across that churchyard to the shade of that cedar tree. You have to remember that to a small boy, the 50 feet or so across that churchyard could seem like 100 miles if he was pulling his sister who weighed, oh, as much as 45 pounds.

So when the two of us reached the shade of that small cedar tree, it was like an oasis in the Sahara, and the tree represented solace from the sun and a respite from the travails of a journey filled with struggle and sacrifice. It was joy we shared — a joy created by a tree.

A few years later, I delivered oil (kerosene) to tobacco barns to be used in the curing process. I remember driving up to a barn in the heat of the summer and finding the farmer and his mule resting under the shade of a big oak tree. It was the only tree in the field that surrounded the barn. The farmer sat under the tree as the mule stood with his head hanging down. The farmer poured some water for the mule into an old hubcap, and then he took a drink for himself from a big gallon jar. As I approached him, he offered me some of that same water, and I took it — out of the jar, not the hubcap.

As we sat there in the shade of that oak tree, the farmer talked to me about the year's tobacco crop, his family, and the college his son was going to attend that fall. The tree was his stage, a venue for expounding on his life — his failures and his triumphs.

That cedar tree in the churchyard of my youth has been pruned back considerably, but it's still standing. Its small size, however, doesn't diminish the importance we gave it when we were utilizing its shade. After all, we were small then, too.

A few days ago, I drove down the dirt road that led to that old tobacco barn where the oak tree had stood. The tree and the barn are gone, and so is the farmer. But the time I spent with a man who allowed me into his life for just a short period is still a vivid memory.

The connection between my life and the people who shared those two experiences with me was a tree. I'll bet neither the Sierra Club nor the paper company ever thought of that kind of tree.

Whatever Happened to Civility

It is with some sadness that I note the passing of what had come to be known as "civility." I don't mean social graces like table manners and that sort of thing. Civility is the attitude itself.

We North Carolinians have been known to be polite people. Growing up as I did in the small-town, rural South, there were certain things I was taught about how to deal with people. Most of the guidelines have some basis in the Scriptures that we'd learned in Sunday school. I expect that's where my parents got their guidelines and where their parents got theirs, and if it wasn't gospel when they got it, it became gospel by the time they told me about it.

Of course, there's the Ten Commandments right off the bat. There are all your basic guidelines right there handed down by God himself to Moses, who will forever look like Charlton Heston to me. After you get past some of the really strict "thou shalt not's" like "thou shalt not kill," it all boils down to treating everybody with the respect that you expect them to show you. That's where civility has gone out the back door.

I always thought that if you met a funeral procession coming toward you on the highway, the respectful thing to do was to pull over to the side until it passed. That's a sign of respect for the family of the deceased. I don't see that very much anymore. A Yankee friend of mine said that was a "Southern thing."

I always thought that children should never "talk back" to their parents, particularly in public. I heard a lady in the grocery store the other day tell her adolescent son to push the shopping cart for her. With a bunch of folks standing within earshot, he told her the cart was too full for him to push; she'd have to push it herself. If I'd said something like that to my mother when I was that age (or any age), as soon as I could have picked myself up off the floor, my mama would have further publicly humiliated me right there in front of all those people by giving me a proper spanking.

Despite growing up with some rough and tumble characters in the log-woods and sawmills, as well as listening to the raucous and sometimes extremely colorful language of men plowing mules, I rarely, if ever, heard a man use foul language in front of a lady. Now, not only do I hear men talking like that with ladies present, I often hear the ladies using the same language.

There's a particular Southern phrase of instructions my mother would use when my sister and I would leave the house. After reminding us of the time we were to be home, she would always say, "Y'all be sweet now, ya hear?" That phrase is the greatest instruction for civility ever uttered. It encompasses all the Ten Commandments and probably every statute in every law book ever written.

Given the fact that the Ten Commandments may not be posted in a public building anymore, I think it would be extremely meaningful to have that most civil approbation written over the door of every courthouse: "To all those who enter here, 'Y'all be sweet now, ya hear?'"

The Joy of Solitude

There's something to be said for solitude. Now, solitude is not the same thing as loneliness. Solitude is being alone and liking it.

For me, solitude is a rarity. The nature and routine of my life puts me with other people all the time. Usually, I like that. I like to talk to people. I like conversation. But every once in a while I like to be by myself.

The first thing I have to do when I want to be alone is find the right place. Unfortunately, there aren't all that many solitary places anymore. A place of solitude has to have some inaccessibility. In today's world of four-wheelers, helicopters, and all kinds of all-terrain vehicles, there are fewer and fewer places that people can't get to.

My wife likes to go to the beach. I don't. I get very little pleasure out of sitting out in the sun until my skin is blistered and covered with gritty sand. Day trips to the beach are out, although occasionally, I do enjoy spending time in an air-conditioned condo overlooking the ocean.

So I have to create a place of solitude. A few years ago, when my son had graduated from college and moved out of the house to be on his own, I transformed his old bedroom into an office/writing studio/hideaway. There's no phone or television in the room. Its primary asset is its relative inaccessibility. It's on the second floor at the top of some very steep, narrow stairs. Only a very important reason can cause anyone to make the climb.

But even that seclusion is not solitude, which leads me to the conclusion that physical separation does not constitute solitude. Solitude is a state of mind that's enhanced by separation from other people not other things.

That ideal solitude allows me to temporarily remove all of myself from the turmoil of this time and place. There is place in the hay barn replete with the smell of the hay and the animals — a place, sometimes warm even when the cold and wet weather drips and blows around it, that offers that respite. In that quiet place, I am alone but not "lonesome," separated from the world but still in touch with it.

The sound of a chicken clucking as it searches for a grain of food; the snorting of horses standing quietly in their stalls; the purr of a kitten as it rubs against my leg; the steady, tiny splattering of rain drops falling from the tin roof to a bucket — all these audibles soothe me.

A ray of sunlight that beams across stacks of hay illuminating the little specks of dust floating in the air; a tiny whirlwind, a "dust devil," that inches its way across the barnyard — all paint pictures that my mind can make uniquely my own.

The solitude has served its purpose. It's provided that respite that rejuvenates my mind so that I can again appreciate the company of other people. Sometimes we have to leave the hustle and bustle of our everyday lives so we can appreciate more fully all that is around us.

In the Tracks of Daniel Boone

Conservation of our environment is a big topic today — and jus-tifiably so. Our natural resources seem to be dwindling faster than we can replace them. Unfortunately, sometimes folks get the impression that many of our fellow North Carolinians are not fully committed to conservation, particularly our wildlife. I don't think that's really the case.

Most North Carolinians have a strong connection to the land. We may no longer toil in the fields, but our roots are there. We return to the land in many ways. Some have small farms or maybe a vegetable garden. Some raise cattle or horses just to look at them and handle them.

Perhaps the biggest misconception concerns hunting and fishing. I really believe that most hunters and fishermen in the state want to conserve as much wildlife as possible. There are large memberships in organizations like Ducks Unlimited, the North Carolina Wild-life Federation, Wildlife Action, and the North Carolina Wildlife Foundation, among others. State government is greatly involved. There are almost as many laws governing hunting and fishing as there are for the operation of an automobile, and most hunters and fishermen understand that unless they act responsibly, their source of recreation will disappear.

But beyond the practical concerns of hunters and fishermen is a more spiritual connection, a bond that goes back to our ancestors. Some of today's hunters and fishermen roam the forests, woods, lakes, and streams not only in search of the wildlife, but also in search of their own life.

I saw him walking yesterday in the tracks of Daniel Boone,
Up yonder where the Yadkin flows
In the glow of an autumn moon.

He walked with the bear and the dear, and none walked in fear,
And the leaves stirred,
And winter's breath drew near.

I saw him walking yesterday in the swamps, in the wet,
        the dark and the gloom.
He paid no mind to the gators and snakes 'cause they gave
        him plenty of room
'Cause the swamp was theirs where they'd shared a
        mutual womb.

I saw him yesterday cookin' over and open fire.
To catch the biggest fish had been his heart's desire,
And when his catch was placed or'e that flaming bier
He'd proved to his friends he wasn't a liar!

I saw him walking yesterday when he heard the rustle of quail,
They flushed from the brush; his dog was on their tail!
But he gazed long at the birds as they rose
And watched as they took sail.

Now they say Ol' Daniel's gone to where there's elbowroom,
That the woodsmen and the hunters spell the wildlife's doom,
But I believe Ol' Daniel's blood still flows in their hearts today
'Cause I saw them walking side by side in the woods just yesterday.

A Taste of Crayon

Back in the day when folks played parlor games (even if they didn't have a parlor), there was often a particular question that would come up as part of the game: "If you had to lose just one of your senses, which one would you choose?" That choice occurred to me the other day as I was driving down the road and saw a sign with a drawing of a pumpkin on it. I realized that the sight of that pumpkin stirred my other senses of smell, touch, and even feel. But those were not what I thought of. I thought about crayons.

Each year when I was a little boy in school, around Thanksgiving and Halloween, we'd always draw and color pumpkins. Coloring pumpkins requires a lot of orange crayons. After drawing and coloring all those pumpkins, my mind filled not with the smell of pumpkins but with the smell of crayons. The smooth touch of the crayon seemed to linger on my cramped fingers. I licked the crayons to dull the color, and I could still taste them on the end of my tongue.

But there was one other intangible feeling I remembered from coloring with those crayons. There was a calmness and serenity that came with the activity. Of course, that feeling is nostalgic now and perhaps not a realistic memory. Nevertheless, just thinking about coloring pumpkins replaces more serious thoughts that usually occupy my mind. It also causes me to think about more sensuous (not sensual) activities.

When I was in fourth grade, there was a field of broom straw behind the school building. During recess, some of us would play in that field. On a few occasions, I'd go away from my classmates and lie down in the broom straw so no one could see me.

If the sun was shining, it would warm me as I lay in the broom straw, hidden away from the wind. I would feel the dampness of the grass under me and smell the sweetness of the straw. I would hear the wind blowing above me, and I would hear the soft swish of the grass as it swayed back and forth. Above me I would see the sky and clouds. The sky wasn't always blue, and the clouds weren't always white, but it all provided a canopy, a shelter. All that combined with the sun and the solitude gave me a feeling of contentment that I haven't experienced since.

If I had to choose one of my senses to live without, I would still be hard-pressed to make a choice. The touch, smell, sight, taste, and sounds of life are the essence of life itself. I know that folks who do not have one of those senses adjust to it, but I'd rather not have to make the adjustment.

I guess what remains for me as I grow older and some of those senses begin to fade is to get a box of crayons, lay down in a field of broom straw, and color pumpkins.

friends and neighbors

Brothers Are Special

I've never had a brother. Not a real, live, blood-kin brother. I've had friends who were so close we could have been brothers except we had different parents. I've always thought that not having a brother was a deficit in my life.

I have a sister who could not be any closer. But brothers are special.

All of this comes to mind because I saw a photograph recently of two brothers sitting on the pier at Lake Waccamaw. Their backs are to the camera as they look over the lake. The two boys sit very close together in the fading sun of a summer day. Their hair is wet, and one of them has put on a shirt against the coming chill of evening. They're not looking at each other, but you can tell they are sharing a unique moment that only brothers can share. I envy them.

As I look at them, I wonder what secrets they share. They are small, and the world they share is so small that things that you and I would pass off as insignificant are very important to them. And things that we might think important are really not very important.

For instance, to little boys, girls are unimportant. At least compared to a bicycle that runs properly or how long you can hold your breath under water. Hitting a baseball is important. It's not until they reach their teenage years that getting to second base takes on a whole new meaning.

And when a guy reaches that new level of awareness, that time when the opposite sex is obviously opposite, a boy can't tell other guys he doesn't understand what's going on. But he can tell his brother. He can even ask for his advice, and he knows that his brother will not lie to him.

Somewhere along the line there may be some sibling rivalry, particularly if the brothers are close in age. But even when they have differences, they are their differences and shared only by them, and only woe will come to any one who should come between them.

I don't know if the poet Oliver Goldsmith had a brother, but I think he must have because he wrote this:

Where'er I roam, whatever realms to see,
My heart untravel'd fondly turns to thee;
Still to my brother turns with ceaseless pain,
And drags with each remove a lengthening chain.

I just think brothers are special.

The Legacy of Mr. Sam

et's just call him Mr. Sam. That wasn't his real name, but he'd be embarrassed if I let his real identity be known. You see, Mr. Sam was a modest man who never did like to draw attention to himself. He was also what folks called "contentious." That means that his disposition ran from grumpy to ornery. He didn't have a whole lot to say to folks, and that just added to the opinion that most folks had of him as a grouchy old codger.

Of course, Mr. Sam wasn't always old and probably not always grumpy. He started out as a young man working on the railroad. He didn't work as a porter, either. He was a section hand, one of those fellows who went out everyday and kept the tracks repaired. It was tough, demanding, physical labor that didn't pay too well.

He lived not far from Hallsboro, a bustling little sawmill town at the time. I only knew him after he had a family of six children — three boys and three girls — and a wife who worked as a domestic for the owner of the lumber company.

He didn't own a car nor even a mule and wagon. He and his family walked everywhere they had to go. Naturally, they didn't go very far, usually just to church on Sunday. More importantly, the children walked to school everyday. He even built his house with the proximity of the school as a major consideration.

School was very important to Mr. Sam. He knew that if his children were to better themselves and make a better place in the world for themselves than he had, they had to have a good education. I heard his children talking in my family's store about how their father made them study at night — and how he would sit right there with them until they had finished their studies. That was remarkable persistence on his part since Mr. Sam never learned to read and write himself.

I remember him coming by the store on his way home from work to buy some items. He'd be covered with the grit and grime of railroad work. I could tell he was tired from the strenuous labor, but he always stood straight, looked everyone in the eye, and was eager to be on his way. He seemed to have an important mission to accomplish.

Mr. Sam's mission was to make sure his children made something of themselves. To the observer, it seemed like an impossible mission given the circumstances, but to his eternal credit, he accomplished what he set out to do. All of his children not only graduated from high school, but also went on to college, and some of them got advanced degrees. They realized their father's dream.

Mr. Sam earned all he could, saved as much as he could, and taught his children about honest work. He instilled in them the values they would need to become contributing members of society.

Mr. Sam's achievement with his children is remarkable in itself, but there are some circumstances that make it even more so given the attitude of so many today. You see, Mr. Sam was a black man in the 1950s. He never thought his children were less qualified to achieve success because of the color of their skin, and he didn't think anybody owed them anything they didn't earn.

Mr. Sam left a proud legacy not just in the achievements of his children, but also in the minds of all who knew him. He was a man who was not afraid to face challenges, a man who stood straight when others bent to adversity, and a man who never acknowledged anyone better than himself nor asked any quarter in fighting for his goals. What may have seemed a grumpy disposition was really just a determined single-mindedness.

High Tea with Barbecue and Hushpuppies

I've always respected and admired Southern ladies. There's something about women raised in the South that gives them a kind
of gentility that puts everybody around them at ease. At the same
time, there's a certain toughness about them that allows them to
rise above whatever depressing circumstances might come their
way. I knew a lady like that when I was growing up.

My family owned a small oil distributing company from the
1950s until the late '80s. Back then, most of our business was
providing fuel to tobacco farmers in the summer to fire their
tobacco curers, and in the winter we provided kerosene or fuel oil
for home heating. Miss Hazel was one of our winter customers.

Miss Hazel was a real lady. She lived in a big, two-story house
that at one time had been a real showplace. It was kept up nicely,
but it had deteriorated some since its heyday back in the '20s. The
Great Depression had affected her family much like others around
the country, and they had sought other ways to provide for themselves. Her husband had died right after World War II, and I never
did figure out how Miss Hazel got her income. I know she was
a substitute teacher sometimes — and she was very careful with
her money.

But even in her diminished financial situation, Miss Hazel never
lost her sense of "respectability," the dignity of her place in society,

and that ability to make everyone she met feel as if they were the most important people in her life at that particular time.

Each fall Miss Hazel would call the oil plant and remind us it was time for us to fill her oil tank. I was usually the one to make the delivery, and almost always there would be some small maintenance of her heating equipment involved.

She had a very elegant dining room with a large fireplace at one end that had been covered with plywood with only a hole for the flue from a standing oil heater. On one delivery day she wanted me to fit that flue into the wooden cover. I told her I'd have to put a flue collar on it to keep the metal from touching the wood. This did not fit into Miss Hazel's esthetic ideals: She had painted the wooden cover a dark blue, so now she instructed me to paint the flue and the cover dark blue, which I did.

I filled the fuel tank, installed the flue and the collar, and painted them both a royal blue. That was not exactly the shade of blue Miss Hazel wanted to match the blue of the satin upholstery of the dining room chairs. I assured her that when the paint dried it would match.

She said, "Well, William, it is time for tea anyway so why don't we have a bit of tea while we wait for the paint to dry?"

I was standing there with oil and soot all over me, but I knew you never said "No" to Miss Hazel. So I washed up, and in just a few minutes she returned with a silver tray and two glasses of iced tea. "Now, William, I have some chocolate cookies or some of those little crackers if you'd like, but just between you and me, why don't we have just of bit of barbecue and hush puppies that I bought yesterday?"

So we did. Miss Hazel and I sat there for quite a while talking about my plans for college. We talked about Emily Dickinson and Walt Whitman and Thoreau. Then we talked of "The War," not World War II but "The War of Northern Aggression." She talked of her father who had fought in that war and when he came back after the war and how he had built the farm back up. Then I will always remember what she said: "Then there were those other wars, but I don't remember them so much."

When we had finished our barbecue and hushpuppies, she noted that the stovepipe needed another coat of paint. I applied it, and she was satisfied.

She moved from the old house some time ago, and it finally fell into ruin. Since then I've had some great sweet tea, barbecue, and hushpuppies, but it's never been quite the same.

A Monument for Percy

A ll of us comprise a community. Some folks' contributions are more evident that others because they get more publicity. And there are others less known who make real contributions, too. Percy was one of those folks.

Percy lived in Brunswick County, right on the edge of the Green Swamp. He moved there back in the late '30s, "before the war." I met him in 1970 when I worked for Reigel Paper Corporation in the woodlands division.

Percy lived in a community that was small in population but covered a lot of territory. And, as is the nature of things, the number of inhabitants decreased as death wound its way through the trees and bogs, the snakes and alligators, and the occasional angry neighbor.

In those early years, many of the men who worked in the swamps — some planting trees, some harvesting the trees, and some draining the swamps for better forestation — had no family with them. At times, the community was comprised of single individuals who lived alone and died alone. Percy was one of those solitary men, but he felt he was a part of each man he met and they were a part of him. So he took it upon himself to take care of those individuals when they died.

When I met Percy, he was an old man. He had long ago retired from his job in the swamp and turned his full-time attention to taking care of a small burial plot not far from his house. It was a community cemetery, simply the final resting place for many of those men who had worked with Percy and been a part of his life.

Percy took me there one winter day and pointed out each plot marked with a single marker made of cypress — a long-lasting wood abundant in the nearby swamp. Some of those markers had deteriorated, and Percy had replaced them with another wooden marker. He couldn't afford a stone, but he thought the wood that had been such a part of all their working lives was appropriate to mark their resting place. He had carved the name and date of each man's death into the wood. He didn't know their birthdays. He kept the little plot cleared of weeds with a sling blade. He said the noise of lawn mowers didn't respect the dead, and he couldn't afford one anyway.

I never returned to that tiny community or saw Percy again and hadn't really thought about him until the other day when I saw a sign on the old savings and loan building in Whiteville that said "North Carolina Museum of Forestry." I think Percy would have been proud of such a venture, such a monument to the industry of which he had been a part.

Percy knew a lot about monuments.

Love Those Carolina Girls

Throughout my life I've had the good fortune of being associated with extraordinary women. Being born and reared in North Carolina gave me the unique opportunity to benefit from the tutelage of women who set a style that is both envied and emulated by other women around the world.

I'm speaking, of course, of "The Carolina Girl." There are several distinctive classes of Carolina Girls, all of them worthy of our admiration.

The first one that comes to mind is the one we hear about in the beach-music songs. She's always tan and is almost always smiling and talking to people, some of whom she has just met, as if she had known them all her life. This Carolina Girl will lie on the beach in full makeup including eye shadow. Despite the heat, she'll never sweat, and her makeup will never run. As the night overtakes this Carolina Girl, she can be found shagging to the music of The Embers, then later sitting or standing barefoot on the dunes or a pier dressed in a bright-colored sun dress, her hair blowing in the ocean breeze and the moonlight shining on her like a spotlight from heaven.

Then there are the Southern Belles, the ones who go to the private schools and have their "coming out" parties, maintaining a tradition as old as the families from which they come. In my youth I met these young ladies at garden parties, chaperoned (as best they could) by their parents as the enticing young ladies executed intricate plans to escape the restrictions of the chaperoning. Beneath the poised and polite exterior beat a heart determined to "let the good times roll"— with a certain amount of decorum, of course. Despite their best efforts to the contrary, these girls never forgot their mamas' instructions: "Always remember that you are a lady." Even as they flirted with us, they always made us country boys remember, too.

There is another Carolina Girl that often gets overlooked — the Good Ol' Girl. She's the one we've known since we were little boys — the one who used to play baseball with us, go hunting with us, or go fishing off the pier at the beach. She never pretended to be anything she wasn't. She was often called a tomboy because she shunned the party dresses and the slumber parties, opting instead to go to the ball games with us.

Then one day she grew up, and she was no longer one of the boys. She fell in love with one of those hunting buddies, and they got married after high school. She works in town as a secretary or as a waitress at one of the restaurants. She's got a good family, intends for her children to go to college, and makes sure they're in church every Sunday.

She's the foundation of the small towns that cover this state. She's the one who makes sure there's food for the church dinners and goes to all the Little League baseball games. She's the Girl Scout leader that helps out part-time at the school. And every once in a while, she'll go fishing on the pier at the beach.

Think about the Carolina Girls you know. I love 'em all.

The Passing of Southern Gentlemen

There is a breed of man indigenous to the South, and the breed is fading away even as we speak: the Southern Gentleman. There are other species that seem to have overtaken this old breed, those that have a higher profile in the eyes of society. The subsequent diminution in recognition is contributing to the demise of the species. The Good Ol' Boy and even the Redneck are better known — they get more attention in the media.

But I believe the Southern Gentleman will endure. The characteristics that have stood him in good stead all these years are the characteristics that can survive. In fact, the true Southern Gentleman seems to flourish in his semi-anonymity. Modesty is one of his most apparent characteristics.

The Southern Gentleman may be the last bastion of masculine gentility to be found anywhere. He abhors the boastful demeanor that so many see as an expression of the male's grasp of his role in society, a role perceived as being just slightly removed from Cro-Magnon man.

He's as much at home driving a pickup truck as he is behind the wheel of a Cadillac. A Southern Gentleman does not feel the need to make other people aware of his status in society. Instead, he chooses to let his daily interaction with his fellow man speak for him. He appreciates his neighbors for each individual's own attributes regardless of his race or social background.

There's much of the Renaissance Man in the Southern Gentleman. He has a broad interest in everything around him. He's appreciative and curious about the sciences and the nature of the world. He appreciates both the biological and the esthetic intricacies that comprise the universe. In many cases, he is a "son of the soil," a man tied to nature for his very existence. Subsequently, he is a religious man who has a strong faith in God and relies on that faith each time he plants a crop.

He doesn't confine his athletic pursuits to the cumulative memory of sports statistics, but he appreciates the skill and effort that goes into achieving those statistics. He is aware of the need for the human body to reach and maintain a certain level of fitness, if only for the body to function at its maximum potential.

A Southern Gentleman appreciates the arts and is involved in some aspect of creativity that allows him to express the beauty of the language or languages we speak and the sights we see and the sounds we hear. Such an activity is not seen as unmasculine but an expression of the God-given talents we all possess.

A Southern Gentleman has an appreciation for education that goes beyond his own personal achievements in that area. He's committed to education as a means of improving the individual and in so doing improving society.

All of this belies the stereotype of the Southern Gentleman as the master of the manor, content to sit on the veranda of his plantation house, sip bourbon, and talk about race horses. Neither does he portray the scion of the "New South," the man whose major role in life is the accumulation of wealth and power. He can be found most often in the small towns where the quality of life is defined more by the Sunday morning church service than the maneuverings of the boardroom.

These gentlemen are fading away. Each week I am reminded of their passing as I attend more funerals of such men. I am sorry to see them go. We'll probably never see their like again, and we will all be the lesser for it.

It will remain for those of us left behind, those of us born in a different time and in a different environment, to not merely revere the Southern Gentleman as a memory of a bygone era but to continue to honor his legacy by emulating him.

And The People Said 'Amen'

If anybody were to ask me what the one common denominator was for every North Carolina community — from the mountains to the sea — I would have to say it's the church.

I don't know for sure, but I would be willing to bet that we have more churches per capita than any other state. Although predominately Christian, many other religions are here, and Baptists and Methodists seem to be the largest denominations.

The role the church plays in the community goes beyond theology: It's often the social center. This was particularly true in earlier years when there were not many other options for social interaction and, indeed, not many other venues for entertainment. Church picnics, gospel sings, and even revivals gave the people in the community the chance to come together not only to worship but also to visit with each other.

The first date with a girl I ever had was at church. It was a youth revival, one of those events that went on all week. After working up all the courage I could muster, I sat beside Rosalie on Wednesday night. She didn't think it was a real date, but I thought it was, even if I didn't get to sit with her the rest of the week.

In some communities, particularly the black community, the church has been the focal point for social, even political, action. The church was the incubator for change. It's attachment to social change brought in many who otherwise would not have found a ladder to climb out of the hole of social injustice.

But whatever it's function, the church is still the spiritual center, whether it be the small, rural churches or the urban mega-churches. It still continues to bring people together to worship, and that's a very personal thing.

I wrote a play once called *The Eli McCorkadale Sales Company*, and in the play Eli recollects on a visit he made to the church of the black lady who helped raise him. I borrowed from the style of poet James Weldon Johnson to tell that story.

The Benediction
He said, "We come this mornin' to thank you, Lord,
For the sun, the sky and the earth,
For rain and growin' things,
And for Jesus the Christ Child's birth.

For your love that comes when we need it most,
On the wings of the dove bird's song.
For food and drink and a place to sleep
When the day's been hard and long."

And the Preacher said, "Amen."

Then the old man slowly stood,
For his back was stooped and bent,
But his voice rose like a trumpet's sound,
His words were heaven-sent.

"Oh, Lord," he said, "I don't ask much,
Just a little food and such,
So when I ask you, Lord, to bless us all,
To cleanse our hearts of fear,
Please listen, Lord, just hear my plea,
As closin' time draws near.

"I've toiled long in your vineyard, Lord,
Worked hard in the boilin' sun,
Now I'm old you see,
My row is almost run.

"But I thank you, Lord, for the life you give me,
For the chance to live in this land.
Now, if you will, I beg you please,
Bless the rest of 'em, too, if you can."

And the deacons said, "Amen."

Then the Sister stood to raise her voice,
In praise of His Holy name.
In her robe of white,
From the front of the church she came.

A hush fell over the church just then,
As The Sister began to sing.
And her voice soared high, so high,
Made the windows and the rafters ring.

Her voice praised God with a passion rare
Heard only in a heavenly choir.
It was filled with joy and heaped with care
And burned with a fervent fire.

Then her voice got soft, she whispered her song,
As tears filled her I she sang,
"Oh, Lord, It won't be long."
The whisper through the rafters rang.

And the choir said, "Amen."

Then they all stood up in one accord,
Swept up in The Spirit's spell.
Their voices rose like an angel choir,
As their song began to swell
And it filled the earth with Peach and Love
"All is well. All is well."

And The People said, "Amen and Amen."

Everybody Needs an Anchor

Almost inevitably, certain people come to mind to remind us of particular times and places in our past. As I thought back over the last half-century of my life, Paul Yoder came to my mind.

In the years that I knew him I never called him by his first name. He was always Dr. Yoder. He was the chairman of the music department at what was then Campbell College (now Campbell University) when I was a student there. In fact, my freshman year was his first year at Campbell as well. He was not what I expected a music professor to look like. He was a big man standing more than six feet tall and with a tendency to be a little heavy. When he walked, he appeared to plod. He took big steps, his big feet landing at a 45-degree angle from his body. His hair had begun to thin, and he combed it straight back. Because of the wispy nature of his hair, it never seemed to stay in place very long.

I had only been on the Buies Creek campus a few days when I happened to read a notice on one of the bulletin boards notifying students that wanted to join the Campbell Choir to come by Dr. Yoder's office for auditions. I'd always liked to sing, so I just went in the music building (a connected group of old Army barracks) and right into Dr. Yoder's office. He was sitting there at an old upright piano and greeted me as I opened the door.

After I told him I wanted to audition for the choir, he got out an old hymnbook and told me to sing "Amazing Grace" as he accompanied me. After that he told me to sing the tenor line as he played.

Then he picked out a song I had never heard and asked me to sing it. I couldn't read music, so I asked him to play it through one time. He did, and I sang it back to him just like he played it. He laughed and told me to report to the choir room the next day. I was to be a part of the Campbell College Touring Choir.

For the next four years, I sang with that group. I learned a lot about choral music — about how to sing and how to create music. I even thought at one time I would become a music major but after a short (very short) tenure in music theory class, Dr. Yoder convinced me that I needed to consider another vocational endeavor. But he kept me in the Touring Choir. I was sometimes the only non-music major in the group, and the people in that choir became some of my closest friends.

I guess the reason I think back on Dr. Yoder now is because he gave a very naive, untutored country boy from Hallsboro the opportunity to experience music and travel. More importantly, he allowed me to become a part of a group that gave me some sense of self-worth that I didn't have, a sense of accomplishment and recognition.

Although he was always supportive, he was very frank with me. If I didn't perform up to my potential, he would tell me in no uncertain terms that I "stunk," and my grade in that particular area would reflect his opinion. But he never let me quit. At one point, I became so frustrated that I went into his office to resign from the choir. He told me to go ahead but if I did to never speak to him again. I stayed.

Even after I graduated, Dr. Yoder and I stayed in touch. For a period of time, I worked for Campbell University and saw Dr. Yoder almost everyday. He became my friend as well as my counselor.

Each year there are other young people who leave the small towns of North Carolina and go on to the institutions of higher learning. I'm sure that many are just as dismayed as I was by the changes that take place in their lives when they leave the comfortable confines of family and familiar surroundings.

But I wonder how many are as fortunate as I was to have someone like Dr. Yoder to provide an anchor in the turbulent sea of academia. How many will find a mentor to guide them? Are there any more like him around?

The answer is yes. There are still teachers who care about their students even as the pressures of "bureaucratic education" surround them. They will make their presence known to those who need them, and I hope those students will seek them out.

Sleeve Garters in a Fertilizer Warehouse

Sunlight shines through several small, dingy windows casting beams of light through the clouds of dust. The dust is swirling, and there is a lot of movement of men pushing heavily-loaded hand trucks through all the melee. But what makes the scene so surreal is the image of a man standing calmly amid it all.

The man is fairly short, maybe five-and-a-half feet tall. He wears rimless spectacles and stands motionless with his arms folded. Although the summer temperature in the warehouse is above a hundred degrees, he's wearing a tie and a long-sleeve, white shirt — with sleeve garters. The sleeve garters are not an affectation. He's a broad-shouldered man with short arms so his sleeves are a little long. The garters bring the cuffs up to his wrist.

The incongruity of the scene is really a reflection of the personality of the man. He's standing in a fertilizer warehouse in a small North Carolina town in the 1950s. Selling fertilizer and other farm needs to the local farmers is his business. But he brings a dignity and sense of decorum to the position. To him, his job required a certain amount of aplomb. It was not a conceit, not a matter of considering himself any better than any of his customers. It was a role that he played that he found consistent with the time and the place.

He wore a coat and tie everyday whether it was at the store, in the field, or at church. He didn't own a short-sleeved shirt. He said there was no such thing as a short-sleeved dress shirt. Every shirt was white and starched to the point that the heat and humidity of summer days before air conditioning never wilted the collar.

He was a country store owner in the days when a country store was the financial center of so many rural communities. His customers could buy everything from fine lace to hog feed. Farmers would come to the store in the spring and sign a "chattel mortgage" to get the supplies they needed to plant their tobacco crop. I remember one such mortgage document that listed "one black mule, a wagon, one good milk cow, and a sow and six pigs" as collateral. During the summer and through the winter, those customers would charge everything to their account, including food and clothing. Then each fall they would come in and pay off that mortgage after they sold their tobacco.

To Mr. Dave, as he was known, an image of a man dressed in a dignified suit and tie exuded confidence, a confidence that his customers could see. They needed to know that the store, in the incarnation of Mr. Dave, would be there regardless of the vagaries and vicissitudes of the farming business. Lord knows there was little enough certainty in farming anyway; there had to be some anchor.

Most of the farmers who signed the chattel mortgages couldn't get a loan at the bank. Mr. Dave believed in his customers, and they believed in him. In all his years in business, he only foreclosed on two mortgages, and, even then, they were five years past due. Times have changed. Nobody does business that way anymore.

Mr. Dave Council was my grandfather. He died fairly young while I was still in college. But I remember him for many things.

He smoked a pack of unfiltered Kool cigarettes everyday, read his Bible every night, taught the men's Sunday School class every Sunday, and always arrived 15 minutes early for church. He was a man of regular habits who believed in hard work, cared about his neighbors, and loved his family. He had a great faith in his fellow man. He believed that people were essentially good. He believed that he should provide an anchor in a stormy sea of farming.

I remember my grandfather every time I drive through the back roads of eastern North Carolina. I always see abandoned country stores, their false fronts weathered grey, the old porches sagging and window panes broken. I see the old screen doors with the faint imprint of the Merita bread logo still visible. There was a time when those stores were the center of a thriving community and the storekeeper kept them all together.

And he believed that you should always wear a tie with a long-sleeved white shirt — with sleeve garters.

Dusty Portraits

Funny thing about dust. It's seldom needed and even more seldom wanted, but it's often available to just about anybody, always comes in abundance, and it's free. A recent long, dry spell has created dust everywhere: on cars, on porches, on flowers and shrubs, and (more often than we'd like) on our clothes.

The absence of moisture has made many of us look for a cloud not with a silver lining but loaded with rain. I'm sure there are rain dances, prayers for rain, and just plain wishes for rain.

Despite all the acrimonious comments about the absence of rainfall, there are some things about the presence of dust that can be positive — depending on the circumstances.

Scientists tell us that the presence of dust in the air is responsible for the beauty of the sunset. I don't know just how much dust it takes to reflect the right amount of sunlight in a way to make the sky God's canvas, but I do know that human efforts to capture the result usually fall short of doing it justice.

I watched several colts playing in a dusty pasture the other day. It was almost dusk, and the rays of the sun were streaking through the leaves of the pecan trees in the pasture. As the colts casually jogged past the trees, a small cloud of dust followed them. When the streams of light struck the dust cloud, the colts seemed to be silhouetted as fog-like apparitions appearing from some painter's Gothic imagination.

Two teenagers, a boy and a girl, were standing at the back of a van in the parking lot at Wal-Mart. They could have been a modern-day Romeo and Juliet as they stood facing each other, holding hands and looking around to see if anybody could see them. They probably didn't think about proclaiming their love for each other through servants and priests or taking poison or stabbing themselves in Shakespearean fashion. Instead, they just wrote their names with their fingers in the dust that covered the back of the van.

A combine harvesting a field of soybeans proceeded unimpaired through the field leaving behind stubbled ground where the soybean plants had stood. It was a great example of technology overcoming nature. That one machine could harvest many acres in the course of the day while it had taken months for the plants to reach maturity. So it was almost like some kind of revenge to have a giant, dusty mist obscure the machine as it slowed to make a turn at the end of the field. Nature had overwhelmed technology for just a moment.

On one of the occasional dirt roads in the state, I saw an old pickup truck moving quickly toward me. I could see the plume of dust behind it and immediately walked far enough away from the road that the passing cloud wouldn't overcome me. As I watched it pass me, I saw that the back of the truck was loaded with furniture: a bed frame, a mattress, and a couple of chairs. Those household elements would be covered with dust when they reached their destination. It did sort of remind me of the black-and-white pictures I had seen of families from the 1930s leaving Oklahoma as the dust swirled around them.

Although these were all scenes that painted vivid but dusty pictures, I still wish it would rain.

– CHAPTER THREE –

down the road

Listening to a Carolina Sunrise

Three sights make the heart of a Carolina boy beat just a little faster. (Well, four, counting the sight of a Carolina girl.)

First, there's the sun coming up out of the ocean off Topsail Beach on a bright summer morning and the wind blowing the sea grass just enough to remind him of the way that girl's hair looked on the beach yesterday. Even in the sunlight, there still lingers a memory of music wafting through the night sky, his fingers touching her fingers as they danced to the music of "My Girl" or "More Than a Number."

He can smell the salt air, maybe even detect that distinctive but not totally unpleasant funk that tells him its low tide on the sound side. As he watches the sun rise, so rises the anticipation of another day at the beach.

Then there's another sunrise in a Carolina boy's memory, the one he sees across the top of a tobacco field. The mist rises to meet the sun looming over the textured, dark green expanse flanked by tall pines. An aroma of tobacco gum and pine rosin, the dusky smell of dust still damp with the dew of late summer fills the air. The breeze carries that Carolina perfume of tobacco curing in the barn beyond the trees.

Another sunrise is the glow of a new day spreading across the top of the mountains; low clouds and morning fog mingle with the smoke of chimney fires as the shadows of the night give way to the light of day. Even in the summer, a coolness requires a coat or sweater to keep a body from shivering, while the sight of mother bear and her cub warm the soul.

Three sunrises speak to the heart of a Carolina boy like me. I listen to the land as it talks and sings. It plays its melodies through the pine trees, whispers through the coves and hollers, and screams up the mountaintops.

It's a voice that ripples over the rivers and creeks,
Wanders down the dirt roads
And through the city streets.

The Carolina boy listens to the sounds;
He soaks in every part,
Then writes down all he hears
In the corner of his heart.

"Hark, the sound of Tar Heel voices..."
The chant of the auctioneer,
The church choirs singing shaped-note music,
The piano played by ear.

It wafts across the cotton fields,
Consoling weary backs,
Lingers in the sawmills
Where the saw don't cut no slack.

It wraps itself 'round abandoned barns,
Like kudzu on the run.
Then it changes tone like a fiddler does
With the setting of the sun.

Dusk coos like a mourning dove,
Soft and Sweet and Low.
The Red Bird sleeps in tall pine trees
Waitin' for the rooster's crow.

The nighttime sound is soft and bright,
Like moonshine in moonlight.
The calmness of the evening sky
Waits the coming of daylight.

I listen to it all.
It's the sound of you and me,
Of farmers and store clerks,
And those that used to be.

It's the heartbeat of our being,
A plea to keep us free,
For tomorrow comes a-rollin'
On each wave that leaves the sea.

A State of Contradictions

It's a good thing I have the chance to meet so many people who are moving into this state from other places. It keeps me aware of the elements that draw them here. Sometimes the attraction is something those of us born here take for granted: four distinct seasons of the year (even if fall and spring are brief), mountains to the west and the ocean to the east, big cities and small towns, and boiled peanuts. OK, so boiled peanuts may not appeal to most of the people moving here, but I still count them as a great asset.

But we also have the undefinable attraction related to the people who live here now and those who created our history. We're a diverse people who happen to share that special distinction of being Tar Heels. It must be something intangible, some indiscernible cultural peculiarity that sets us apart from other sections of the country.

Perhaps it's that very contradiction that provides the commonality. We're at once a part of the New South, as evidenced by the development of Charlotte as a financial center of the country, while down the road, the farms that have been so much a part of our heritage still populate the Piedmont's rolling hills and the flat lands of the Coastal Plain. The Research Triangle Park is a reflection of our quest for technological advances while the mountains echo the beauty of our natural heritage.

Almost within sight of the towers of finance and technology lies the residue of memory, of a lifestyle that portrays the same drive and determination shared by farmers, scientists, and financiers.

Those early settlers had the same desire to build a life for themselves and their progeny on those farms as do those who now inhabit the offices on Tryon Street in Charlotte, Elm Street in Greensboro, and Hillsborough Street in Raleigh.

I believe, like fellow Southerner R. Scott Brunner, that perhaps drive has been refined over time, tempered collectively by our own peculiar quartet of regional afflictions — war, weather, want, and willfulness. We've simply exhausted the capacity to distinguish the sublime from the ridiculous. That's what makes us unique, that gives us our unique humor. That may be the one element of our culture that tempts so many to join us.

On the one hand, where else could those who choose to join us find such a tremendous desire to improve the education of our young people but also find one of the lowest per capita expenditures per child for education in the country?

Where else could they find a place with such a traditionally strong work ethic and so many unemployed as the old manufacturing giants of furniture and textiles close and the family farms disappear?

But where else could they find a flourishing arts community in every town, large or small? Or youth baseball programs unsurpassed anywhere in the country? Or a growing emphasis on developing tourism by building on the very heritage that brought us to this point? Or conservation programs aimed at preserving the natural environment that has been so much a part of all of us?

How often have we seen pickup trucks parked at the country club? Or fancy restaurants serving black-eyed peas and collards? Or bluegrass music played at a debutante ball? Or guys at a beer joint taking up money to give to the Baptist church to send to tsunami victims?

Rather than impair our progress, I think these contradictions elevate us to a higher plane, one on which the extremes converge and inhabit us, comedy and tragedy. That may be what makes us the studies in contradiction that we apparently are to those outsiders who choose to join us but who do not understand from whence we came nor what it means to be where we are.

Going With the Wind

During the Fourth of July holiday, I took a couple days off and went to the beach. I'm not really a "beach person," but my wife is, so whither she goeth, I will follow.

One reason I don't particularly like to go to the beach is the heat. Although I'd rather endure extreme heat than extreme cold, I don't prefer either. For that and other reasons, I usually look forward to rain at the beach. That was certainly the case that week as the temperature hung around the 90s and the humidity hung even heavier.

I like to watch it rain anywhere when I can sit under shelter and feel the wet wind and smell the rain as my body begins to cool. Like most beach houses, the one where I was staying was set up high off the ground, so I could actually sit under the house and enjoy the rain.

I should've known, however, that the sound of distant thunder was a portent of more than a summer shower. By the time the rain and wind swept across the beach where I was, it had reached full thunderstorm proportions. The wind was blowing so hard I couldn't find a completely dry place to watch the feisty weather, and visions of past hurricanes ran through my mind like an old newsreel.

I watched the water rise in the driveway and inch its way under the house/carport where I was. The flashes of lightning forewarned me of each blast of thunder, but I was still awed by the sound and the fury of the storm. The thunder seemed to crack the sky with each blast, causing a rift through which the rain would fall in bigger and bigger torrents like a lake bursting through a dam.

That close encounter with nature's fury was relatively short-lived, miniscule in time and violence when compared to a hurricane. As the wind died down and the rain turned to drizzle, I thought about the way we so often look at wind.

The wind carries a certain amount of poetry in the way it makes us aware of our emotions. Sometimes we're afraid as we see the evidence of its destruction: debris flying through the air, buildings blown down or away, and waves of water swept up by the wind like the sweep of a child's hand in a bathtub sea.

The wind in other seasons causes different feelings. Autumn winds fill yards with leaves. Spring's blustery winds dip and dive capriciously across the fields and woods, blowing away the winter's chilly blasts and pulling in the warm breezes of summer.

Those warm pulses are the winds of youth, the gusts that blew across the sand dunes and carried the sound of Maurice Williams and the Zodiacs out to the night sea.

As I sat there at the beach after the thunderstorm, I was reminded of a poem from my school days. Emily Dickinson wrote, "Who has seen the wind? Neither you nor I. But when the trees bow down their heads, the wind is passing by."

And so it did on that stormy day at the beach.

Making a Courtroom Fashion Statement

I just like old courthouses. There's something comfortable about them. I don't mean comfortable as in a nice place to sit. That is definitely not the case, although the Columbus County courthouse has a second floor porch complete with rocking chairs. I mean comfortable as in reassuring and stable.

Part of the courthouse appeal is the fact that it's the center of the community in many cases. Among other things, it may be where we get our marriage license, copies of our birth certificate, records of property we own. Sometimes it's also where we go to get divorced and pay taxes.

There may be some folks who have never been in a courtroom. That's a very fortunate person, not only because they have not run afoul of the law, but also because they haven't been exposed to what I believe is a public display of disrespect for the law and the judicial system in particular.

I'm not talking about the people who stand on the courthouse steps and burn the American flag. I'm talking about the people who show up in the courtroom dressed as if they were going to the beach or working in the field.

I was standing in the lobby of the courthouse the other day and saw some folks dressed in cutoff jeans going upstairs to the courtroom; one had on a T-shirt with no sleeves, and all of them wore flip-flop sandals. They weren't handcuffed, so they evidently had time to go home and change clothes.

I don't know what brought those folks to court. I assume they had to come. If they were there as witnesses, I'm sure the prosecution hoped they were there for the defense and vice-versa. I certainly wouldn't want someone dressed like that to testify as to my character.

I mean, I certainly don't think it's absolutely necessary for a man to wear a suit to the courtroom or even a sport coat and tie, but he should at least be neatly dressed in clean clothes. Ladies don't have to dress like they're going to church, but they shouldn't look like its disco night in the courtroom either. Unlike some of the prisoners who are brought in from the jail in those orange jumpsuits, most folks have an option.

I don't think you can judge somebody's guilt or innocence by the way they're dressed, but how a person is dressed when he comes to the courtroom shows his attitude toward the court. A neat, clean appearance shows respect not just for the judge and his court, but also for the system of justice which allows every one a chance to be in that courtroom and receive a fair review. That's a pretty good reason to clean up.

I don't know if the judge let those flip-flop-wearing people in his courtroom. Maybe he required them to wear those orange jumpsuits as an alternative to the T-shirts and flip-flops.

Like Coming Home

Some time ago I went up to Newton Grove in Sampson County to speak to their Committee of 100 annual meeting. The trip there and the occasion itself made me a mite wistful.

I took a circuitous route, which took me first to Lumberton then to Fayetteville then to Newton Grove. It was probably the time of day — late afternoon — that made me remember why I'm so glad North Carolina is my home.

When I turned off Interstate 95 onto U.S. Highway 13, the sun was lingering over the tops of the pine trees. With the sun setting behind me, the fading light showed me pictures of life as tranquil and poignant as a pastoral scene hanging in a museum.

Fields, freshly plowed under after the recent harvest, stretched open and flat, the marks of the discs running like lines on a wrinkled sheet of gray paper.

Acre after acre of cotton whiteness stood in stark contrast to the shadows cast by the surrounding woods. It looked as if the clouds of the daytime sky had descended to earth to rest for the night.

I saw some children playing in the yard, burning off that last burst of energy before supper. It was a scene of innocence; a reminder of that spell of life before responsibility sweeps the innocence away.

Sampson County is still mostly rural, reflecting the lifestyle that's so much a part of our heritage. There are certainly bigger farms now, but there are still many smaller farms that have yet to yield to the pressures of economy. Given that heritage, it was appropriate, I thought, that the meeting I was to attend, a meeting that addressed the economic concerns of the future of the area, was held in a small, country church fellowship hall.

When I stepped into the meeting room, I immediately felt at home. The ladies of the church were preparing a wonderful meal: ham and peas, homemade casseroles and corn bread, and other food that smelled and tasted like home. And, of course, there was plenty of sweet iced tea, along with cake for dessert.

The folks that gathered for that meeting are like folks in so many other communities across North Carolina: hard-working, salt-of-the-earth people who want to do things together to make their communities a better place to live.

After I ate the delicious food, a group of singers from the host church, Hopewell United Methodist Church, sang. The singers were all men who seemed to really enjoy what they were doing, and the lady who played the piano bound them together like a family. Most of them were kin to each other, a fact that probably added to the quality of their singing. They sang some familiar songs, some songs of the church, and some gospel songs — songs whose harmonies whispered and shouted of faith and glory. They were the kinds of songs that made me want to sing along with them, so I did, kind of under my breath.

After the business came my turn. I gave my usual talk, sharing those things about North Carolina that make it such a special place to live. While I was talking, I realized that I was looking at what made this state special: people like those in Newton Grove and the hundreds of other similar communities across this state. It made me proud to be a part of it all.

Our Music Defines Us

I have said on many occasions that music is and has been a major part of my life. I believe that most people could say the same, whether they realize it or not.

Music is not only a personal means of expression but also reflects the social makeup of the people in any given geographical area. Unfortunately, some people use that reflection to build a less-than-flattering stereotype. Just as there are all kinds of people in this state, there are all kinds of music.

For most people growing up in North Carolina, the first music they heard was usually the music they sang in church. The best thing about singing congregational hymns is that individual singers can sing without feeling that they are being heard. Everyone can sing for the pure joy of singing regardless of the talent of the singer. Sometimes the result of this perceived anonymity is not totally appreciated by fellow singers.

Sometimes that need to sing results in a unique blend of voices that may produce a sound not completely in keeping with the sound the composer originally had in mind. That's when the appreciation for personal expression must override other considerations.

The second source of music we hear usually comes from the radio. During my youth, before the advent of FM radio, many local AM stations had local musical groups performing live in the studios. Those groups ranged from gospel to country and some "hillbilly" music now referred to as "bluegrass." The quality varied, but the venue allowed those who wanted to sing for an audience the chance to do so. The movie *O Brother, Where Art Thou?* has a very accurate depiction of how that type of performance might have been.

So far, what I have described seems to support the stereotype that many folks have of music in the South and, particularly, North Carolina. But our musical meanderings extend beyond a single genre. For every guitar and banjo picker sitting on the porch perfecting his art, there's another artist sitting down to practice the piano, or sing scales, or practice the flute or any number of instruments. From these students will come the concert artists, jazz ensemble players, choir members, opera singers, and, possibly, rock stars.

But that's not the whole picture either. Music doesn't have to be performed for an audience to be appreciated or enjoyed. Every musician takes his music personally. For the woman who sits quietly in her home in the mountains and plays the soft ringing sounds of the dulcimer, for the mother singing unaccompanied lullabies in the early morning hours, for the young guitarist sitting on the sand dunes composing songs for his sweetheart, for the teenagers with all the amplifiers plugged into the garage outlets, and for the individual who sits in an apartment filled with the electronic equipment that reproduces all the sounds of music, the experience is personal. A fellow named O'Shaughnessy once said,

> "We are the music-makers,
> And we are the dreamers of dreams,
> Wandering by lone sea breakers,
> And sitting by desolate streams.
> World-losers and world-forsakers,
> On whom the pale moon gleams;
> Yet we are movers and shakers
> Of the world forever, it seems.

Music is part of our culture. It's not just a reflection of who we are but is in itself very often who we are. So when somebody tells me that we're not a very "cultured" society down here in this part of the country, I have to ask them to listen more closely.

The Sound of The South

I heard a fellow playing a banjo the other day, a solo. He wasn't a professional musician, but he seemed to enjoy what he was doing and didn't care whether interlopers like me appreciated the effort or not.

Listening to a solo banjo performance is unusual. It may be because a banjo player likes to kind of play off other instruments. But listening to this fellow strum and pluck a banjo as he sat in the shade of a pecan tree gave me an appreciation for that most American instrument.

Some folks will tell me that the banjo came to this country from Africa, and that may be. But I associate the music of that instrument with this country, particularly the South. That's where it became popular and where most banjo music as we know it originated.

As the man played that banjo, my mind began to form images created by the music. When he began to pluck the strings one at a time, he was slowly creating a melody that didn't flow as much as piqued my interest, causing me to anticipate the next note.

This was music, not of the honky tonks and bawdy houses or even concert halls, but back porch music created by untrained musicians who spilled their souls into the instrument and sent forth a profusion of emotions — sounds of lost love, loneliness, and sorrow. What you might call the blues. In fact, a lot of folks do call it the blues, and it's part of America's music: jazz.

Then the man stopped his plucking, took a sip of some beverage concealed in a paper bag, and, without looking to see if anybody was watching, began to strum that banjo with such enthusiasm that you expected to see the strings pop right off. He moved his left hand up and down the fret board while his right hand kept the rhythm going full speed. His whole body seemed caught up in creating that music. His foot was moving rapidly up and down, and his head was moving from side to side, all in perfect beat with the music.

When he completed his song, I went over to where he was seated. As he took another drink from the paper bag, I introduced myself and asked him where he learned to play like that.

"I didn't exactly learn," he said. "It just kinda come to me from listening to other folks play."

I asked if he played with a band. "Naw. I just go my own way. Most of what I play don't nobody else know anyway. I make up most of it."

With that he went back to his playing, oblivious to me and others who stood at a distance to watch and listen. I didn't stay much longer; I felt like an intruder. This man was playing solely for his own enjoyment. He didn't seem to care that others were listening, and he didn't seek their approval.

As I think back on that man and his music, I believe that both represent the South. The sound he created was uniquely his, but he had absorbed much from those who had gone before him. Just like the South.

The Peach Connection

Every once in a while something will happen that reminds me that there's still some good left in the world.

I was coming back from Charlotte and decided to stop at a roadside produce stand. Actually, I had been instructed to stop at that stand and buy a specific amount of peaches for my wife and my mother. Since this particular stand also sold the most delicious homemade peach ice cream in the world, I felt that as a good husband and son it was my duty to stop here to buy the peaches.

It was late afternoon. Not many people were there, nor were there many peaches. When I asked if maybe they had some more in the cooler, a nice young lady who was grading peaches said her peaches would be ready in just a minute if I wanted to wait. So I took that opportunity to buy some of the aforementioned ice cream.

The ice cream stand was really a corner room of the big sorting shed. Three young ladies were working in the little room, making and selling that delicious peach ice cream. I ordered a cone from the little dark-haired girl who was just as cute as she could be and every bit of 16 years old. She brought me my ice cream cone, and I paid her the $2. I sat down on one of the benches to eat the cone and wait for the peaches.

In a few minutes, a young man drove up in a pickup truck. When he got out, I could see that he was wearing a pair of jeans and a T-shirt. His clothes were clean, and his hair was cut short. The first impression I had was of a typical teenage boy who liked peach ice cream as much as I do.

When he got to the window to order his ice cream, he shyly placed his order while the girl smiled at him and said something that made him laugh. Apparently they knew each other. He paid for his ice cream and got back in his truck and drove away.

The little dark-haired girl watched him leave then told her friends to look at this boy who had just purchased the ice cream cone. She was so excited. That smile seemed permanently attached to that cherubic face as the trio of young ladies watched the boy drive out of the parking lot.

I thought, how nice to see some old-fashioned shyness on the part of the young man and to see such unabashed happiness on the part of the young lady. There hadn't been a single bit of prurient behavior. I was so used to the swagger of over-confident boys and the equally provocative response from the girls that I was a little taken aback by the interaction of this young couple.

As I loaded my peaches into the car and began to drive away, I saw the young man return. He went back up to the ice cream stand and ordered another cone of peach ice cream. But this time he didn't immediately get back in the truck. Instead, he leaned on the frame of the order window eating the ice cream and talking to the dark-haired girl who was obviously glad to see him return. I watched them for a little while as the boy finished his ice cream cone. He then kind of shuffled back to his truck with a big smile on his face. As he drove away, the dark-haired girl was jumping up and down, evidently very pleased with the conversation.

I don't know what those kids talked about, but it didn't have a loud-music accompaniment, and they treated each other respectfully. I liked that.

Now, Who Was Your Granddaddy?

Genealogy is usually thought of as an activity that provides for an accounting of our ancestors, a history of our family, a tracing of our heritage. At least, that's the theoretical definition. In reality, there are some folks who take a different view.

Some folks make up a lot of their heritage as they go along. It's always amazing to me to listen to some folks expound on their family history from one occasion to another. Here in North Carolina, it's not uncommon to find families whose Scottish heritage takes on the trappings of royalty, depicting every clan as directly descended from Bonnie Prince Charlie himself. Surely, there must have been more of the "common people" or else the Prince was an extraordinarily busy and prepotent sire.

Other folks claim high-ranking descendants from various European families, African chieftains, and Asian princes. Ironically, these same folks say we should have stricter immigration laws.

Some folks get deathly serious about their ancestors. They search graveyards (cemeteries to polite folks) looking for names and dates that tell who begat whom and when they did it. Really, kind of private stuff to be writing down for people who might not even be family to read about.

Genealogical searches, however, are usually done by a member of the family being researched. In my family, that person was an unmarried female cousin. Appropriately, Cousin Helen was a librarian, someone not unaccustomed to looking through indices of names and familiar with the methodology of research.

These seekers of pedigree can be found in the register of deeds office, in the newspaper archives, and more recently, on the Internet. They're looking for anything that might shed some light on the family's past accomplishments and failures, some indication that we might have risen from poverty to prominence or fallen from distinction to anonymity. Of course, the real historian is the one who records everything, the good and the bad, without trying to make the history of the family something it isn't. Cousin Helen was a real historian who told the truth, good and bad.

The South has many Cousin Helens. They're usually the ones who instigate and organize family reunions. They're there at church homecomings and class reunions. Those are great occasions for gathering "oral history," those stories of the saints and rascals who preceded us and, for better or worse, set the stage for the rest of us to follow.

Some of us might look for ancestors who established the family as "prominent leaders in the community," while others of us might be more interested in finding out who were the wastrels and brigands, the colorful characters who are far more fascinating.

In any case, the pursuit of family history, while not limited to Southern families, is certainly of concern to almost everyone in the region. And it's not just the "high society" folks who are interested. The activity crosses every boundary of race, religion, and social strata. We all want to know who we were so we might be more likely to know who we are.

We can't choose our ancestors, and that's just as well. They probably wouldn't have chosen us anyway. While we all are interested in where we came from, we should remember that the man who boasts only of his roots is conceding that he belongs to a family that's better dead than alive.

Who Are We North Carolinians?

Several years ago I was involved in a project called "Leadership North Carolina." It's an admirable effort to bring together folks from across the state who have the inclination and ability to make a difference in their communities. A major part of the program is to make the participants aware of just what makes up this state, how it works, who makes it work, what needs fixin', and some suggestions on how we might fix it.

One of the first questions that came to mind the first time I met with these folks up at the class in Boone was, of course, "Who are they?" The primary answer I gathered after spending about six months with them is that they're all very intelligent, well-educated people who "like calling North Carolina home." Many of them are not native-born North Carolinians. But it's a reflection of their intelligence that they moved here as soon as the opportunity presented itself.

As soon as I made the determination that they were all North Carolinians, I was faced with the inevitable question of, "Who is a North Carolinian?"

One of my classmates said that prior to coming to North Carolina he thought the state was made up of hundreds of little Mayberries. Of course, that's not the case. Certainly, small, rural communities still exist today, and they're part of our heritage, a part we want to remember, and, for those of us who grew up in those communities, a part we want to cherish.

But we can't define North Carolinians only by where we live. The geography and demographics are too diverse. There must be something else, some common denominator that makes us all Tar Heels.

First of all, I believe we have a sense of place — we see ourselves as part of a unique tradition bound to the land. We have a proprietary sense of belonging that's been strengthened by a heritage of struggle and triumph, a fierce love of God and family, a collective heart and soul that share a unique history.

We are a friendly folk. It doesn't take long for that aspect of our character to rub off on new arrivals. We have been raised to "act toward everybody like we would like them to act toward us." Even strangers are greeted with, "Hey, how y'all?" People in passing automobiles wave at those who pass them on the highway. Inevitably, when we leave a gathering, it's a gradual process. Our leave-taking involves statements like, "Y'all come back any time, now, ya heah." And, "Tell you mama and them I said hello".

We're all related. North Carolina is one mass, extended family. A plethora of family reunions keeps us aware of our kinship to one another. This adds to that sense of belonging. It also means that because of this sense of family, no one is alone. Someone's always there to help. And they'll help out whether we want them to or not!

We're a gracious people. Having and exhibiting good manners is just something we're taught from birth. Not having good manners paints us as "common" or "trashy," a designation our mothers cast only on the most degenerate souls.

We like good food. We like all kinds of food not just grits and collards, although they rank pretty high on our preferred menu. There's seafood down on the coast, barbecue (in every style), home-cured hams, and, of course, boiled peanuts.

I'm sure there are a lot of other common characteristics that make us all North Carolinians. Native son James Taylor was right when he talked about "Going to Carolina in My Mind." Maybe that's the common denominator. "I think, therefore, I am."

Unfortunately, many of our children have never heard of the official toast of North Carolina. Here it is. Teach it to them. It speaks to who we are, too.

"Here's to the Land of the Longleaf Pine, the summer land where the sun doth shine, where the weak grow strong and the strong grow great. Here's to Down Home, the Old North State."

Big Celebration in a Small Town

Every time I get close to sliding down the slippery slope of cynicism, something comes along that keeps me from falling into the abyss. On the same day that the news was full of dire predictions about the creation of nuclear weapons in Iran, terrorist threats around the world, big-business chicanery, and the awareness that only a relatively small portion of the North Carolina lottery revenue will actually go toward education, the little town of Bath was doing something great.

It was concluding a yearlong celebration of its 300-year founding. Bath is the oldest town in the state, and it has survived three centuries because its heart has always been strong. It's not a big town, but it has a big heart. I saw that when I arrived to speak as part of the closing ceremonies for the celebration.

The elementary school gymnasium was full of people: local, state, and national dignitaries; townspeople; folks who came in from the area; and lots of children. Many of the adults and almost all of the children were dressed in period costumes. Everyone turned out to celebrate.

They had been celebrating all year, beginning with a gathering of the North Carolina General Assembly under a giant tent that got blown down by a tornado. Weather scrapped much of what had been planned for the opening presentation, so the closing ceremonies gave the town an opportunity to show the fruits of a lot of work.

What transpired during that ceremony is pure Americana, a display of community effort that evoked in my mind a Norman Rockwell painting: a presentation of the colors by the local junior ROTC, the pledge of allegiance to the flag, followed by the singing of "The Old North State." The old-fashioned lyrics of "Hurrah, Hurrah, the Old North State forever" echoed through that gymnasium with a resonance that reached out to the Tar Heel soul.

During the ceremony, a small violin ensemble and the school band played, a trio of ladies sang a touching farewell song, and folks thanked each other for the hard work.

I was reminded of the Olympics' closing ceremonies as the children marched onto the stage in the Bath school gymnasium. I will long remember those children walking on stage in their homemade costumes, their riverboat made from cardboard, and the other little vignettes played out as they had rehearsed them, their short lines spoken with nervous voices as their families looked on with pride. There was no grand technical display, no figures floating in air, no special lighting effects. No one had spent millions of dollars to create a giant spectacle, but the result was no less grand.

Years from now when those children are grown, they will look back and remember with fondness and pride their part in celebrating their town. They won't remember that I was there, but I will remember that they were. This was small-town America at its best, a coming together as a community to celebrate all that has created this special place we call home. How lucky I am.

southern ways

Death of a Mule

John Henry Garrison's mule died the other day. The death in itself is worth mentioning since the demise of a mule today is significant given the few that are left living. But it was the notice, rather than the death, of the passing of John Henry's mule that I thought significant.

The mule was known as "John Henry's mule." That name, or lack thereof, tells you something about not only how folks felt about the mule, but also how John Henry thought of the mule. Sometimes in the South mules take on a sentimental value because they represent a nostalgic past that surpasses any reality. But there was nothing sentimental about John Henry's mule. The mule was strictly utilitarian; he didn't need a name.

"I bought him to plow my garden with," John Henry told me. "I had a good tractor. but it was too big to plow a little plot of ground like a garden. So I got a mule. Bought him at an auction over in Siler City. I had a bunch of plows and a harness that my daddy had left, so I just cleaned it up and put it on the mule. Bad thing about that was, the old harness wore out pretty soon, and I had to hunt all over the place to find a replacement. Never did get it all alike, just a piece here and there to get by."

The first time I saw John Henry and his mule I was visiting a man from Sanford, and we went to look at an old house next to John Henry's. We saw the man and mule plowing next to the house we wanted to see, but we didn't approach them. It's best not to interrupt a man while he's plowing. However, as we were walking around the house John Henry came up and introduced himself, just checking on any visitors to the place. The owner lived elsewhere, and John Henry kind of kept an eye on it for him.

Having always had an interest in mules, I commented on what a fine animal he was working. "Yeah, he does pretty good," he said. He went on to tell me about learning how to plow since he had never really worked a mule before. "I always thought this stuff about plowing straight rows was just some of my daddy's bragging. But I tell you the truth; it's a real accomplishment to be able to plow a straight row. Helps if the mule already knows how."

We left the house, John Henry, and his mule and went on back to Sanford. I would go by the place many times in the course of the next year or so, and I always looked for the mule. He was usually standing alone in a small, fenced-in area that contained a single covered shed in one corner, and a little pile of hay.

One day when I went by, I didn't see the mule, but I did see a pickup truck parked by the fence. I drove a little way down the road before my curiosity got the best of me; I turned around to go back to check on the status of the mule.

John Henry was there emptying the water trough. When asked about the mule he answered, "Yep, he just up and died."

You ever notice how many things "just up and..." die, move, quit, etc. That's a phrase we Southerners use to describe a lot of things we don't understand or know the reason for happening.

I asked John Henry if he was going to buy another mule. He said he wasn't; they were too much trouble.

As I was leaving I noticed a mound of dirt beside the shed. I assumed it was the grave of the mule. A hand-painted wooden sign lay on the ground beside it. I figured it was to be the marker for the grave. It said, "John Henry's Mule."

Never Trust a Chicken

From time to time my thoughts turn to chickens. Some people might think this is a bit strange, but if you've watched chickens much, you have to admit they're interesting creatures.

The chicken has historically caused humans to consider the basic philosophy of life. A frequently asked question of those who seek to find the real meaning of life is, "Which came first: the chicken or the egg?" This has become such a trite question that we sometimes don't take all the implications of the inquiry seriously.

Once we approach the question, some other considerations come to mind. Does fried chicken taste the same to everybody? How would we ever make that determination? Given the difference in every element of our human makeup, we have to assume that our taste buds have their own personality. But since the taste of fried chicken seems to be universally enjoyed at least to some degree, we have to assume that there is some similarity in the way our taste buds communicate to our brain the actual, real, essential, and elemental taste of fried chicken. To tell you the truth, I don't really think about it that much when I'm eating fried chicken.

I've also had occasion to note the newsworthiness of chickens. Many years ago, I read about some chicken growers — somewhere in Georgia, I believe — who had been disgruntled at the low price they were getting for their chickens. As protest, they planned to parachute a large number of live chickens onto the headquarters of the company that was proposing such low prices. The same article noted that, fortunately, the plan was abandoned as being inhumane.

I was reading an account of the development of community newspapers in this country and saw where back in the early part of the 20th century a small-town paper in Louisiana had once printed a story about a dog that was raising two chicks (biddies) under the house of a local farmer. It didn't mention what it was feeding them, but stranger things have happened in Louisiana. It leaves one to wonder how long it would be before the dog's maternal instinct expired and the chicks became dog chow.

In the same journalism textbook was a photograph that had appeared in a Batesville, Mississippi, newspaper. It showed a woman displaying an egg and a sweet potato, both extremely elongated. The caption read, "Last week, Mrs. ____ visited the newspaper office with an extra large hen egg, which later proved to have a double yolk, and an unusually long sweet potato." Not only was the newspaper desperate for a story about natural phenomenon, but also the sentence structure added to the uniqueness of the egg.

As much as I like chickens and admire their individuality, I would find it very difficult to have a chicken as a pet. You can't give them a name. Think how ridiculous it would sound to stand out on the back porch and call your chicken. "Here, chick, chick" is about as good as you can do.

But the main reason I can't develop a relationship with a chicken is I can't ever get one to look me in the eye. Chickens are just not trustworthy.

Dr. Scarlett O'Hara

I was looking through some old appointment calendars the other day and noticed the number of festivals and other celebrations that I've had the good fortune to be a part of over the years. Many of those festivals have included beauty pageants, for which I emceed. Admittedly, the number of participants in those pageants has declined in recent years.

That's not to say that there aren't still plenty of young ladies who enjoy getting all dressed up, working on a talent presentation, and doing all the other things that will allow them to ride in parades, cut ribbons, and generally remind us that Scarlett O'Hara still lives.

Beauty pageants are a typically Southern tradition. The popularity may have decreased nationwide but not so much in the South. The restructuring of some contests, like the Miss America Pageant, is supposed to make the business more relevant. And I guess it will. But hundreds of small towns still celebrate everything from vegetables to water and want to select the perfect young lady to exemplify the ideals of the community.

Despite the protestations of feminists and other progressive groups, there's no lack of eager participants for the contests. Philosophically, I believe it has something to do with the Southern soul. Every Southern boy, whether he's a good ol' boy or an urbane sophisticate, still sees the perfect woman up on a pedestal, radiant in a sequined gown, waving and smiling, allowing her subjects to marvel.

Sometimes in the course of the pageant, it becomes apparent that the parents or the girl's friends have played a major role in getting the girl to enter the pageant. She's in it for the fun of it, just to be a part of the group, and winning isn't her real goal. Such was the case in a pageant I emceed several years ago in the Piedmont section of the state.

Back then a part of the competition required the contestant to come out on the stage in her evening gown and walk around a little before approaching the emcee who would ask the girl a question prepared by the judges. The girl would be judged on how pretty she looked in her gown, her poise, and how well she answered the question.

This particular young lady had been having a great time during rehearsals, and I could tell she was in the event just for the fun of it. But her "on-stage" question was serious. She had told the judges during the interview process that morning that she intended to go to college after graduating from high school with the ultimate goal of becoming a doctor. (Being a doctor or a television journalist are the two big occupations for a lot of pageant contestants.) So when she came out for her evening gown presentation and interview portion, I read the note I had been given by the judges.

"You said earlier that you planned to go to medical school and become a doctor. Going to medical school will involve a considerable amount of laboratory work and may necessitate your working with a cadaver. How would you feel about working with a cadaver?"

There was a long pause. The girl asked me to read the question again, which I did.

Then she said, "I know that becoming a doctor is a challenging goal. I haven't really had a lot of experience yet in working in a laboratory, but I pride myself on being able to work with anybody, so I guess I could work with a cadaver. Besides, two heads are always better than one."

Miss Scarlett could not have said it better.

Festival Folks

North Carolina is known for its festivals. And with good reason. We have so much to celebrate. Almost every weekend there's a festival somewhere in the big towns, little towns, and even some rural areas that don't have an official spot on the map. But they all have something to celebrate.

One weekend I was pleased to be asked to be a part of The Barbecue Festival in Lexington. Of course, there was plenty of barbecue and other food along with a variety of entertainment and vendors. The crowd was tremendous; somebody estimated 50,000 people. Every vacant space in town was rented for parking, and there were lines of people everywhere.

The people attending the event were the biggest entertainment. Watching the masses reaffirmed my previous observations at similar gatherings: Crowds are just a large collection of individuals.

The festival folks had kindly set up a booth for me to sell and autograph books along one of the busy areas not far from the site of an excellent beach band. During the course of the afternoon, I noticed some unique individuals.

There was an old man in a denim coat — one of those long denim coats with the big pockets. It was a fairly warm day with high humidity and the threat of rain. Despite the incongruity of the coat and the warm weather, it was the rest of his attire that got my attention. In addition to the coat, he wore a sweater, a flannel shirt, a pair of plaid Bermuda shorts, and sandals with socks. Go figure.

A lady came by the booth, picked up one of my books, and began to leaf through it. She asked if I was the author, and I told her I was. She continued to look through the book. Then she began to read each page and chuckle a little. "I like this," she said as she continued to read. "This is the kinda stuff I like," she commented. She stood there for almost 20 minutes reading the book. "Keep up the good work," she said as she walked away without buying a book.

A teenage girl came by. She had tattoos over almost every visible part of her body, and much of that area was also pierced. She picked up one of the books and asked, "Is this free?" I said, "No, they're for sale. Would you like to buy one?"

"No thanks," she said. "I was looking for something free to give my boyfriend."

A lady came by with a plastic bag full of stuff. She bought some cookies from the booth next to mine then walked over and looked at the books and the sign the publishing company had provided. "Do ya'll make anything?" she asked. "No, ma'am," I said. "We're selling books. Would you like to look at one?"

"No," she said. "I'm looking for something useful."

There were other interesting people who passed by but didn't stop for conversation: a man in a business suit, incongruous among the people in much-less-formal attire, with an umbrella tightly rolled and ready for the rain; another man in an obvious hurry stopping at each booth for directions to the nearest bathroom; and a young mother with three small children, each on a separate leash.

The best question of the day came from a lady who bought a cookie from the booth next door, turned to look at the crowd, and, with a bewildered look on her face, asked no one in particular, "Where did all these people come from?"

For the Love of a Peanut

From time to time I feel compelled to talk about boiled peanuts, especially when somebody asks me what's so special about them. I take that as a challenge to once again explain my feelings for one of God's greatest creations.

There are some who say that boiled peanuts are not fit to eat. Those who say that are usually born north of Raleigh and were introduced to this wonderful delicacy at a late point in their lives. My grandson was born in Charlotte. His father was born in Chicago and, although he has lived in the South long enough to have acquired the taste, he refuses to accept boiled peanuts for the epicurean delight that they are. Therefore, I feel compelled to introduce my grandson to his cultural legacy as soon as he is old enough to chew solid food.

Boiled peanuts are the caviar of Carolina cuisine. It's a part of our culture as unique as shagging at the beach or making homemade ice cream at the church picnic.

Eating boiled peanuts has been an integral part of our lives. There's a special joy in pulling the plants out of the moist soil and savoring that aroma that portends the taste to come.

Every boiled peanut lover has stood anxiously by a pot of boiling water filled with raw peanuts and periodically scooped out one or two to see if they were ready. The anxiety of waiting for the peanuts to simmer in the salt water was a test of will power.

For many of us, some of our most cherished childhood memories include boiled peanuts. Many of our grandmothers introduced us to the peanut-boiling process as they prepared the nuts in a big iron pot set over an open fire in the backyard. After the long wait for the boiling and simmering, we were treated to big bowls full of hot peanuts. We ate the big ones first, sucking the tasty salt water out of the shells, and the "pops" that had no peanuts weren't eliminated!

Peanut boilings served as the cause for us all to get together. Sometimes it was for a song fest, where we would all gather around the piano, maybe with a guitar and a banjo, too, and sing songs from the hymnbook or that we had heard on the radio. Some would sing while others ate peanuts.

When tobacco was cured in wooden barns and somebody had to stay up all night to feed wood to the furnace, neighbors would come over, boil peanuts, and sit around and tell stories.

It was always a sure sign that the tobacco market had opened when the peanut boys were set up on the street corners downtown and you could hear them hawk their wares all the way down the street.

My first trip to the tobacco market meant that my father would buy me a Pepsi and a bag of boiled peanuts, then place me on top of one of those neatly stacked piles (not loose-leaf sheets) of tobacco there in the warehouse and tell me to stay there until he got back. I was glad to do so.

Boiled peanuts are still around. You can find them in most of the convenience stores all year round, thanks to modern refrigeration. Every once in a while in the summer, you may see a vendor set up a roadside stand where the peanuts are being boiled in stainless steel cookers that look like the remnants of a liquor still. Then you can buy them hot.

Real boiled peanut connoisseurs cook their own peanuts at home, eat as many as they can while they're hot, then put the remainder in freezer bags to store until Christmas, when they'll bring them back out to warm up just to tide us over until summer's return.

The price of a bag of boiled peanuts has escalated considerably since I was a boy. I paid over a dollar a bag for hot peanuts the other day. Hot boiled peanuts. Worth every cent.

"If You Miss the Train I'm On…"

I miss the trains. I miss the sound of them, the rumbling of the earth as they pass, and the diminishing noise that fades into silence as they disappear into the distance.

Many years ago they took up the railroad tracks in Hallsboro, and life for me and the other residents there hasn't been the same.

One day, I recalled that sense of awe that I used to get from watching the train pass. I had stopped my car at a railroad crossing near Hamlet as a train was going by. It was one of those long, long connections of boxcars. Since I couldn't see the front or the end of the train, I decided to get out of my car and see if I could still feel the rumble and the roar.

Sure enough, there was a great roar. The noise seemed to sweep over me. The speed of the passing boxcars enveloped me. I was reminded of the cliche tornado survivors use to describe the approach of the storm, "It sounded just like a freight train comin' through!"

In a way, I was as swept up by that moment as if I were in the midst of a tornado. I was aware of the size of the procession, each car almost the size of some mobile homes, as they flashed by me like earthbound rockets. I felt so insignificant standing there as the lettering on the sides of the cars blurred into an incomprehensible stream of meaningless graffiti.

Then came the caboose, and I watched it recede down the track. The noise grew fainter until it was replaced with that silence that seems so deep in contrast to the recent clatter. I remained standing in the middle of the empty road. I could still feel the passing of the train even as the sight and sound disappeared.

Trains are a big part of our lives, whether we're aware of this fact or not. The development of trains parallels the growth of this country and is an indicator of the changes that have taken place. Much of the transport of goods is now by truck. Long-distance passenger travel has shifted to airplanes and automobiles. Things change.

Maybe trains are still around because there's something romantic about trains. They generate visions like trips on the Orient Express in pursuit of some foreign spy or the idea of hobos traveling free across the countryside. There's even a certain amount of romanticism attached to watching a train from the loading dock of a railroad station in a small North Carolina town on a summer's day and waving at the engineer as he roared by. I wish I could do that again, but I can't. They took up the tracks.

Our Moonshine Heritage

For the first 50 years of my life I never saw or attended a stock car race. That's a strong admission from a fella who prides himself on his North Carolina heritage.

I was certainly aware of that racing heritage, however. I recognized the names of Junior Johnson, Lee and Richard Petty, and Fireball Roberts, and I had seen the movies *Thunder Road* with Robert Mitchum and *The Last American Hero*, the fictionalized biography of Junior Johnson. Still, I had never been to a real race.

I went to my first race in 2001. I was prepared to hear a lot of noise as I watched all those cars make left turns for three hours. I was pleasantly surprised to find out there was much more to the race. Fortunately, a friend of mine who accompanied me to the race was a real fan. He explained the rules of the race to me, and I discovered that, like any other sport, if you understand the rules it makes a lot more sense.

Since that initial race I have been following the sport more closely. I have discovered that the sport whose beginning was in the North Carolina mountains as part of the moonshine business has now expanded far beyond its regional appeal into one of the largest sporting industries in the country.

Nascar, the billion-dollar organization that oversees the sport of stock car racing, is big business. But as I watched the race and the fans around me, I could feel the same excitement that was there at the beginning, at the dirt tracks and older venues like

North Wilkesboro and Darlington. The old spirit is still there if we look for it.

No headlights shown through the darkness,
Only moonlight to guide the way.
They'd deliver their load to Charlottetown,
Before the light of day.

Somewhere along the darkened trail,
In hiding waited The Law.
The two would come together,
In the greatest race you never saw.

The dust rolled and sirens wailed
Searing the mountain night.
The Chase was on, God turned His head,
'Cause neither man was right.

They dueled 'round the curves and hills
And up the mountainside.
The engines roared together,
As Death raced side by side.

Somewhere in the darkness
The Devil dealt the hand
And the revenuer left the mountain
Headed for the Promised Land.

The moonshiner headed on down the road,
Now a solitary way.
He'd make it in to Charlottetown,
Before the light of day.

In another time and another place
The race would take up again,
A race run with hundreds of cars
Driven by driven men.

They'd make more money than he ever got
For all of his moonshine,
But they'd race with a passion shared,
As they headed for the finish line.

The men now racing 'round the track
Aren't haulin' mountain dew.
They're chasing a dream of fame and fortune
Attained by very few.

But each time you sit at that track
And thrill to the race and the crowd,
Look up; you'll see that moonshiner
Racing through a cloud.

Race on down that mountain road,
With The Law on your back.
Your spirit races on today,
'Round that oval track.

Race on with the dream
Of making one more haul.
Doing the best you can,
That's all. That's all.

I'm still learning about stock car racing. I even had a fella drive me around a track at about 140 miles an hour so I could get the feel of the race. It scared me 'bout to death. I believe I'll just watch from the stands.

Of Kudzu and Wisteria

There are some chores that I like to do alone. One is trimming shrubbery. I like to do this alone because I can go at my own speed, which is admittedly slow and erratic.

The pace is the result of my physical limitations brought on by a lack of exercise and a love of good food. Nonetheless, when I take on the job of pulling wisteria vines and trimming hedges, I enjoy the activity.

The joy of that activity was interrupted one day when a friend of mine saw me working in the yard and stopped to chat. Usually I welcome any opportunity to talk with folks, but when I am hot and sweaty, I am not the greatest conversationalist in the world. Plus, if I stop to talk, I lose my momentum and have a hard time making myself get back to work.

By far the biggest reason I hate for people to talk to me while I'm working in my yard is, frankly, I don't want to hear their advice. I may not be doing whatever I'm doing correctly, but it's my yard and my labor, so please don't give me advice.

The conversation the other day is a good example:

"Hey, watcha doing?" he asked.

Now, it was fairly obvious that I was pulling wisteria vines from bushes that had been overcome with the purple-flowered vines. In retrospect, it's amazing that someone who didn't even recognize what I was doing was an expert on it.

After I stated the obvious, he said, "You know it's goin' to come right back if you don't dig up the roots."

"Well, hopefully, as soon as I can clear away enough of the vines and bush, I'll be able to see where the roots are and dig them up," I replied.

"Whatcha ought to do is just cut everything down and start over. You know, wisteria is almost as bad as kudzu when it comes to overtaking shrubbery," he continued.

"You figured out a way to get rid of kudzu?" I asked.

"Oh, yeah. You just plow it up and cover the whole place with salt. Seems like I remember something in the Bible about God covering the land with salt because it was barren," he said.

"I think you're talking about what the Romans did to the city of Carthage at the end of the Punic Wars," I replied.

"No, no, my friend. There ain't no such thing as a puny war. All wars are big to the people involved."

Here I was standing in my own yard covered with sweat, dirt, and dead leaves and talking with a man who had just proposed that I sow my yard with salt, and this action was based, incorrectly, on Biblical precedent.

I asked my friend if he had any salt with him. He said he didn't, but if I went to Pierce and Company they might have some ice-melting salt left over from the winter. He thought they'd probably sell it cheap since the threat of ice was gone until next winter.

I know William Jolly has had a lot of unusual requests there at Pierce and Company, but I doubt if anybody has ever asked if he had any left-over salt.

I love my neighbors, and I love to talk with folks. But doing so while I'm trimming shrubbery is just not a good time for it.

Travel for the Sake of Travel

After a lifetime of traveling all over the country, particularly North Carolina, one would think that I'd be tired of traveling. Some days that's true, but on most occasions when I get in an automobile, I look forward to once again moving across the landscape, no matter how familiar it might be.

Although I always have a destination in mind, often it's the journey itself I enjoy.

There's something comforting about passing by familiar places, to realize that some things remain the same even as time and the elements may change their appearance. In the course of my journeys, I noted old tobacco barns that are still standing in the same place I first saw them 50 years ago. They're now covered with kudzu; their walls tilted a little, the tin roofs detached by storms. But they're still there.

Many of the little towns I used to drive through are circumnavigated by travelers who follow the faster-moving bypasses and interstate highways. If I'm not in a hurry, I like to go through those old towns where the railroad tracks, not as busy as in the past, still divide the town, and the parking spaces angle like the feathers of an arrow guiding the tracks through the town and out into the flat farmland of North Carolina.

Some elements of the former landscape are more visibly absent than others. The sprawling tobacco warehouses are being torn down, leaving gaping vacant lots to mark the places where so much of the money that built the other buildings in town originated.

So many of the country stores that used to be rest stops for travelers and gathering points for the local residents have disappeared. I used to stop at those places to get directions to a residence or a place of business. The owner was usually there, and he knew everyone in town and in the nearby countryside. I always enjoyed the conversations at these rest stops. They gave me a chance to learn about the people there and what made that little spot on the map different from the next little spot on the map.

That's why I look forward to stopping at one of those old stores that I've frequented all these years. It's a chance to catch up on the news of those families I've come to know, to find out where the little boy who used to sweep the floors and fill the drink box is working now, how many children he has, and inquire about the health of the patriarch who has retired and turned the business over to younger family members.

Much of my traveling is at night. There's that same comfortable feeling of familiarity coming back home on those country roads. The music on the radio and the darkness of the night come together to insulate me, if only for a while, from the telephone and the Internet and the stream of people who want something from me.

Sometimes, as I travel alone on those night roads, I try to recite to myself little slivers of poetry or some lines from a play. One that comes to mind as I write this is from Robert Louis Stevenson, who said, "For my part, I travel not to go anywhere, but to go. I travel for travel's sake. The great affair is to move."

Wanna Buy a Goat?

As I've been driving across North Carolina in recent years, I've noticed an increase in the number of goats I see on the state's farms. You might ask why I'd notice such a thing. Well, there's no real reason apart from the fact that I've always wanted a goat of my own, and the profusion of them has gotten my attention.

I don't have any idea what a goat costs. If it costs much more than a dollar a pound on the hoof, it would be out of my price range. But just because the price may be beyond my pocketbook, that doesn't mean I can get the desire for a goat out of my mind. No, sir. I believe there must be a way for me to obtain a goat without spending too much money or going in debt. It would be most embarrassing to list on my financial statement an indebtedness due to the purchase of a goat.

Therefore, I propose that those folks who have goats for sale and wish to expand their market should look into the possibility of a "Rent-a-Goat" sideline. Rent-a-Goat has many advantages for both the renter and the rentee.

First of all, the renter (someone like me) doesn't have to put up a whole lot of hard-to-find cash in order to acquire the company of a goat. This will allow the renter to use what small amount of money he may have on hand to prepare a place to keep the goat and to buy the necessary feed.

I've been led to believe that goats are easy keepers, that they'll eat what other livestock pass over. However, I don't think it would be prudent on my part to believe the old statement about goats eating tin cans and such. A diet of tin cans wouldn't help me to maintain a goat in the manner that I'd like, and the strain on the digestive system of a goat subsisting on tin cans could cause extreme discomfort if not death.

Under my proposed Rent-A-Goat plan, the renter may pay in small affordable installments rather than a lump sum for the outright purchase. In addition, if both parties agree, the rent can be applied toward the purchase of the goat.

Of course, it depends on the kind of goat being rented as to just how much the rent may be. For instance, a plain female goat (called a doe, not a nanny) who's not bred and has no physical features that would designate her as more beautiful than most other goats, and therefore would be less desirable to male goats (called bucks, not billys), could be rented fairly cheaply. However, a female goat that's already bred or is so beautiful that the chance of her achieving that status soon, could bring a much higher rent. Since desirability is in the eye of the buck, ascertaining the beauty of a goat can be kind of chancey.

I've been told by certain goat authorities that goat traders, as opposed to goat breeders, are an untrustworthy lot. Goat traders have been known to misrepresent the status of female goats, i.e. telling prospective buyers (or renters) that a certain goat is "with kid," while all she really has is a bad stomach ache brought on by eating too many Coca-Cola cans.

I would propose that some action be taken by our state legislature to prevent such misleading practices. A Truth in Goat Trading Bill would go a long way toward legitimizing the Rent-A-Goat business. (It could help the sponsoring legislators come voting time, too. There are a lot of goat lovers out there.)

Of course, the real advantage of renting a goat as opposed to the outright purchase is that if the renter decides that the goat isn't really something he wants, he can just return the goat. Even with penalties for goat wear and tear, it would be a less expensive endeavor than spending a lot of money on a promising goat only to find out goats can be a b-a-a-a-a-d business investment.

Roadside Attractions

Somewhere I remember reading that there's a time and place for everything. I take that to mean that nothing is completely useless. Even the most apparently useless can serve as a bad example.

Over the 50 or so years of traveling throughout the South, I've had occasion to stop at all kinds of places that exhibited unique attractions. There was a time when many service stations would keep some kind of wild animal caged up behind the store, supposedly to entertain those buying gasoline while the attendant (remember them?) pumped the gas.

Sometimes the store would have weird-shaped vegetables on display. I have seen gourds that looked like eagle heads, squash shaped like the Star of David, and tomatoes joined together to look like a spaceship.

Many years ago, I was driving through the Belhaven area and saw an advertisement for a flea wedding. I found a museum there that exhibited a dried arrangement of a flea wedding. All the fleas were dressed and in church. Of course, you had to have a large magnifying glass to see this phenomenon. After I saw it, I had to wonder why it was created in the first place and, secondly, how real to life it was. I mean, you gotta do some research on a project like this.

The research must have been a real task. After all, there are very few flea weddings of record and even fewer photographs. According to a dog I once knew, fleas don't bother with marital vows anyway, choosing to live in sin and multiply in abundance.

The diorama itself leaves a lot of unanswered questions. Upon very close examination, I failed to determine which was the bride and which was the groom. Nor could I tell if the minister was Protestant, Catholic, or Jewish. Having a particular interest in music, I looked in vain for a musician. In fact, it was a very small wedding, literally as well as figuratively. I did determine that there was a best flea and a flea of honor, but I couldn't tell if the ring bearer was a flea or a speck of dust.

While not exactly on a quest, I've sought out other oddities whose purpose is questionable. I remember a store in Craven County that proclaimed and exhibited a self-kicking machine. I'm sure all of us at some time have said, "I felt like kicking myself for doing that." I have — right after I paid to see the flea wedding. Well, here was the solution.

The contraption had four shoes mounted on metal spokes, a hand crank, and a belt to drive it. The main problem I'd have in making use of the machine is operating it effectively. Anyone who wishes to inflict such injury upon himself must be coordinated to a great degree. Each time the shoe kicks you, you automatically stop turning the crank. That means that each kick is a deliberate action that only a masochist can enjoy.

Usually I always say how much I miss the good old days. Not this time.

– CHAPTER FIVE –

the way we were

They Were Playing Our Song

I don't know about other folks, but there's something about music that triggers specific thought processes for me. If I hear a particular song or even a particular style of music, I am transported to another time and place.

Almost everything of significance in my life is related to music in some manner, and hearing music from the past just naturally causes me to reflect on the previous period in my life.

It's always a personal reflection. Most people would think classical music would create pictures of concert halls, big orchestras, or spectacular opera stages. Not for me. I grew up in a small, rural community where I heard very little, if any, classical music before I went to college. And even then, it wasn't in a formal performance that I first heard and appreciated the beautiful music of the masters, of Bach and Beethoven and Mendelssohn, the operas of Wagner ... and Puccini's *Madame Butterfly*.

It was while I was in the music department that I first heard a girl's beautiful voice proclaiming the artistry of one of Puccini's incomparable compositions as she rehearsed for a recital. The walls of the practice rooms in the old music department were so thin that when you walked down the halls when all the rooms were occupied, all you heard was a cacophony of voices and instruments. But one quiet Saturday afternoon I heard a pure, clear soprano voice singing "Un Bel Di Verdremo," and I was captured by the sound. For a while, I was transported from little Buies Creek to 19th-century Japan, and I could feel the anguish of the young Japanese girl as she longed for her departed American sailor.

Now when I hear that music, I don't see grand concert halls but a dingy, dilapidated frame building that had once been Army barracks on a college campus. The beauty of the sound and the remembrance of the music overwhelm the visual image.

Other kinds of music have their respective reminiscences. Roy Orbison has to be heard in old, wooden gymnasiums festooned with prom-necessitated crepe paper to really be enjoyed. Patsy Cline's rendition of "I Fall to Pieces" can best be appreciated when heard on an AM car radio parked at the back of the drive-in theater. The Mormon Tabernacle Choir can't sing "The Old Rugged Cross" as well as a small choir of dedicated parishioners in a country church on Sunday morning in the spring. Dixieland jazz reminds me of summer afternoon garden parties where the girls all wore brightly colored sundresses and the guys wore white pants and white shoes and drank too much.

I'm sure everybody has their own memories of songs, and each song has its own place in time and space. Even those folks who don't "have an ear" for music can appreciate the imagery it creates.

The great American composer George Gershwin said, "Music must repeat the thoughts and aspirations of the people and time."

It does for me, and more.

The Beauty of the Moment

I saw the little boy walking down the road, his head bent down in concentration. I couldn't tell if he was focusing on some small insect on the ground or was weighed down by an event that loomed ahead at school.

The fact that he was walking was significant. Children are usually chauffeured by an adult to a variety of activities: ball practice, dance class, gymnastics class, etc. I never could understand why anyone has to be driven somewhere else to get exercise.

It was early morning. The sun was peeking over the trees, and there was a mist along the roadside and over the soybean field. The boy's somber appearance and the play of sunlight on the morning mist gave the whole scene the feel of an impressionist painting.

But this picture wasn't hanging in an art gallery. This was real, and it was right here.

And while it was unique in that moment, it was not all that unusual for those of us who live out in the country.

Sometimes, I take scenes like I just described for granted. As each season changes, we see the beauty all around but seldom realize just how fortunate we are to be able to see that beauty.

When summer ends, we look forward to the fall and the changing colors of the leaves. The bright hues get our attention, but there are subtle changes that we take for granted. As the cornfields slowly change from green to tan and the piles of peanut bushes cover the field with hundreds of little dark mounds, there is a sense of settling in, a feeling of completion and the anticipation of rest to come.

I wondered if the little boy walking alone down that road the other morning realized how lucky he was. Probably not. Sometime in the future he may look back and remember those scenes. More than likely he's in too much of a hurry to appreciate what's around him now.

I stopped at an old house not far from where I live the other day to take a look at the flowers growing beside the house. It was one of those old domiciles built up off the ground to allow ventilation to get under the house. The paint had long ago peeled off the siding, but the weathered board had not shown any sign of decay. No one lives there anymore, but the owner keeps the yard mowed, so I could move around pretty freely. (Only in small, rural communities can people just walk up unannounced and roam around somebody else's yard.)

At the back of the house was an old garage, and piled under the garage was an assortment of garden tools, all of them rusted and unusable. I guess the thing that struck me most was the sameness of color about the whole scene. The boards were gray; the tools were rusty brown. The scene would have been dismal except for one purple flower that bloomed right beside the wall of the building. It stood out in contrast to its surroundings, more beautiful because it was different from everything else. It bloomed there on its own, unattended and unaided by humans.

The house is on the road that the little boy took on his way to school. He probably didn't notice the flower because, like many of us, he was so caught up in thinking about what was ahead that he missed the beauty of the moment.

What Time Of Year Is It?

Nature sometimes has a way of confusing itself. It's usually the weather that's the catalyst for confusion, the conduit for incongruity.

Fall and winter are good examples. In the dead of winter, we should at least be easing into a comatose state. It's a time when earth's creatures are supposed to take a break. Bears hibernate. Squirrels eat all those nuts they accumulated. Birds fly south. Flowers shed their blooms, and trees shed their leaves.

Warm weather in the winter can certainly be classified as "unseasonable." I saw several things last winter that lead me to believe that you may not be able to fool Mother Nature, but you can mislead her.

One morning I saw a robin, a harbinger of spring, pecking at stray grains of birdseed that had fallen under the bird feeder on my back porch. The sun was shining in a blue sky. That night, the temperature fell to below freezing. In the morning, I saw the poor robin perched on the edge of the concrete birdbath pecking at the frozen water!

All around my house are several pecan trees. As recently as Christmas Day, I saw squirrels scurrying up those trees bearing pecans in their mouths, leaving the nuts in the hollowed out portions of the trees, then — anticipating a long, cold winter — scampering back down for more food. Maybe I was just imagining things, but during a really warm spell, I declare I saw those same squirrels throwing pecans out of their hiding place back onto the ground.

One of the dogwood trees along my driveway had a flower on it the week after Christmas.

Hurricanes were still brewing way after the end of November. (It occurred to me that since we had run through the alphabet in naming that year's storms and since storms always come from the south, we could give the remaining storms Southern double names like, Annie Lee, Betty Lou, Carrie Mae, etc.)

On New Year's Eve, I saw a girl go into Pierce and Company in Hallsboro looking for sun tan lotion. Not only did they have it in stock; they sold it to her at the regular summer price.

In the opposite extreme, I saw a curiously attired fellow walking across the parking lot at the mall in Wilmington. He had on one of those parkas with fur around the hood, and the hood was pulled up over his head so that all you could see was his face. The rest of his outfit consisted of a pair of shorts and flip-flops. Was he so confused that he was just making an attempt to cover all the bases?

I guess that should've told me that we all can be misled by the weather.

Indeed, the clincher came when I saw a car with Pennsylvania license plates stop for gas at a local station. When the driver got out of the car, he was wearing the traditional winter ensemble of many of our northern visitors: a Hawaiian print shirt, Bermuda shorts, black over-the-calf socks, and sandals. When he had finished filling his car with gasoline he took off, due north.

Reunion by the Creek

She called it a "river run," although it wasn't really to a river and we drove instead of ran. It was not unlike hundreds of parties that have been held in hundreds of cow pastures throughout North Carolina. We drove the old pickup down to the creek that ran across Louise's grandfather's farm in Harnett County. It wasn't really her grandfather's farm anymore either. Her grandfather had died back in the late 1950s, but we all still called it his farm although Louise's uncles now owned it.

In fact, there wasn't a whole lot about the event that was like it used to be. Things change a lot in 50 years. What had started out as a kind of celebration of spring by a few college students had turned into a semiannual reunion. I had been invited to attend because I had been assured there would be lots of stories told that I could repeat in my columns.

Since 1958, the group had come back on an irregular schedule and reenacted those early, carefree days. Through wars and financial struggles, personal triumphs and tragedies, the birth and growth of children, and all the other things that make up daily life, they came. They would bring food, ice, some chairs, appropriate beverages, and their memories. Then they would share it all on the bank of the little creek where the bare remains of the old grist mill stood.

It was the ideal place for parties. The site couldn't be seen from the road, and it nestled down beside the creek and between two hills. It was cow pasture all around, but along the creek trees had grown and provided shade for the party guests. Idyllic was the word that came to mind.

Louise told me that during the early reunions some of the guests would go swimming in the creek. Some, like Eleanor and Gwen, had even gone skinny-dipping.

In those early days they would circle the vehicles around a campfire, turn all the radios to the same AM station, and dance. But over the years, the physical activities diminished along with the energy and exuberance of the participants. For the last several years, Louise said that they mostly just sat around and reminisced.

In the years before, Louise's husband, Billy Ray, had come, but he died last summer shortly after the reunion. Sara and Edwin always came, but Louise had heard that Alzheimer's was taking its toll on Edwin. Carolyn usually came, although her husband (who hadn't been a member of the original group) passed away a couple of years ago. Bud and Dudley usually came together. They'd played baseball together in college and had kept in touch even after their wives had died. Then there was Elaine. She'd been the cheerleader, literally and figuratively. She was a cheerleader in school, and it was Elaine who always kept the party going even to the point of leading the group in some of those old cheers.

As we parked the truck and unloaded the folding picnic table, I told Louise we ought to wait for the others. She said they'd be here shortly, and all would be hungry and thirsty. After we got everything ready, Louise turned on the truck radio to the oldies station. We ate and drank and listened while waiting for the others.

We waited a long time. The sun went down and the air turned cool. We built a fire, and still no one came. But Louise was sure they would, so we waited some more. While the music of Maurice and the Zodiacs played in the background and the fire burned down, we danced and laughed.

After a while I told Louise we should get on home; apparently no one was coming. She didn't answer right away, but she started gathering up the food and drink, and I pulled off the tablecloth and folded up the table and chairs. As we got back in the truck I said, "I'm sorry nobody came. I was looking forward to hearing some good stories."

"Oh, they came," she said. "I saw them dancing over by the creek just like we used to. They'll always be there." And so they will.

'Twas the Day After Christmas

W̲hen Christmas is over and we are looking at the New Year, what do we see? Considering all we ate during Christmas, it's probably not our toes.

One of the most treasured traditions of Christmas is feasting. So much of what we do during the holiday season concerns eating: church socials, parties, family gatherings, etc. No wonder Santa Claus is a bit overweight.

The food we eat at Christmas is not conducive to dieting. I have no idea how many calories there are in fruitcake or those little chocolate-covered peanut butter balls or pumpkin pie or turkey dressing or even butter-basted turkey for that matter. I can safely assume that the total amount of calories (or fat grams or whatever it is that adds weight to my body) consumed during Christmas should be enough to last me about a year if I could hibernate like a bear.

However, I can't hibernate. That doesn't mean that my lack of physical activity could not be mistaken for hibernation. Hibernation means "to pass the winter in a torpid or resting state." Other words that come to mind are sluggish, dormant, numb, apathetic, and the dominant phrase, lazy.

Certainly the casual observer could mistake my lack of mobility for the comparable comportment of a bruin ensconced in his winter cave. After a filling holiday repast I do tend to recline in a supine position, close my eyes, and let all that gastronomic intake turn to fat. And, as with the hibernating bear, it's not wise to disturb my slumber. Such a move on the part of family or friend can arouse a wrath not typically seen in my usual amiable state. A wonderful meal and the availability of the reclining chair has to be one of the most sleep-inducing combinations ever conceived. I feel sure that if the aforementioned bear had access to a recliner he would stay in his cave year round.

The likelihood of prolonged inertia is annulled by the ever-present and obligatory "chores." This category of labor is divided into two major subsections: (1) holiday-related chores and (2) regular, everyday chores.

Holiday chores include taking down the Christmas tree. At my house this task is mandated by my wife to be completed no later than midnight on December 26. Failure to complete said task in the allotted time can result in expulsion from the dwelling and/or an intolerable silence that lasts until the task is completed.

It's a fairly simple job to remove the ornaments from the tree, wrap them individually in tissue paper, and place them in a box to be so positioned in a closet that retrieval next Christmas will involve the complete evacuation of the space. The really tough job is removing the lights from the tree. Once upon a time, Christmas lights were red, white, blue, and green and were each about the size of my thumb. Our current Christmas tree lights are all white, very small, and number in the thousands. Removing them from the tree is a major operation demanding tremendous concentration and the dexterity of a surgeon. Of course, no matter how hard I try, the majority of the lights won't be fit for use next year, necessitating the purchase of another thousand or so.

Other holiday tasks include disassembling all the other decorations that have graced the house since the beginning of the season. Since the removal of the tree and its decorations usually puts me in a mood to destroy everything else in my path, "undecorating" doesn't take long. The same can be said of the other everyday chores. If it isn't nailed down, sealed to the house, or otherwise secured, it's thrown away in a manner reminiscent of Ghengis Khan sweeping across the steppes.

Once I have accomplished my appointed chores, of course, I return to my pseudo-hibernation to issue in the New Year.

What I Learned from Scrooge

Sometimes in the days before Christmas I tend to get a little cynical. I know it's not supposed to be that way, but I guess all the commercialism and unhappy situations in the world press on me and I begin to take on the attitude of old Ebenezer Scrooge. When that happens, I take a voluntary look at Christmas Past, Present, and Future, and, fortunately, I see all those time periods come together — the past creating the present and predicting the future.

I see those days before Christmas as:

- Package-laden cars driving past shorn fields of cotton, tobacco, corn, and soybeans.
- Houses with the doors and porches framed with strands of all-blue Christmas lights creating a misguided feeling of an ice-covered landscape far removed from the temperate Carolina winter.
- Deer hunters lining the sides of the road as they look anxiously toward the woods and fields, their guns poised. They are modern huntsmen carrying on a tradition that began as a need to provide food for the winter tables.
- The bare limbs of pecan trees forming a filigree across the winter sky, the fruit of the tree awaiting harvest and inclusion in pies whose recipes have been handed down from generation to generation.
- "Redbirds" perched on porch railings unaware of their exalted

status as "cardinals," official state birds, their color bringing a seasonal contrast to the stark landscape.

- A pseudo-covert gathering of old friends to share some home-made wine.
- The unique, youthful anticipation of children, watched by older folks hoping to become children once more, wishing for the return of that which time and adulthood have worn away.
- Music coming from church choirs as they rehearse for the Christmas cantata, their untrained voices making beautiful notes sung from the heart.
- The taste and smell of the kitchen in its preparation of oyster dressing and ambrosia, culinary treats savored once a year.
- Wood fires burning in fireplaces drawing families together, and wood fires blazing from a steel barrel warming the night for turkey shoots.
- Old friends gathering at oyster roasts, and others gathered at more sedate parties with eggnog and "finger foods."
- Stockings filled with fruit, candy, and nuts along with a small toy, all hung by the chimney late on Christmas Eve.
- The expectation of families sitting in a circle around the room as they take turns opening presents to the accompaniment of "oohs" and "aahs" and "just what I wanted!"
- An unspoken wish for snow on Christmas day.
- And somewhere above it all, through the noise and the revelry, the sounds of "Sweet Little Jesus Boy" and "Oh, Holy Night" reminding us of what it is all about.

That's what I thought about as Christmas approached. That's the way it used to be for me, the way it mostly is this year, and the way I wish it will be next year.

Keeping the Dream Alive

I was trying to think of how I wanted to end this book when I got a call from my granddaughter who lives in Charlotte. Actually, my daughter placed the call since Mia, my granddaughter, is only three years old. (Of course, from a grandfather's point of view, Mia could have placed the call herself.)

She wanted to tell me about her dance recital coming up. At three years old, this was Mia's first performance. I told her I would try to be there, of course.

After I completed our phone conversation, I returned to my thoughts on this book and my emphasis on what we all share as North Carolinians. It occurred to me that by the time Mia gets old enough to appreciate what a great state we live in, so much will have changed that she won't know how much it means to me now.

So I envisioned a conversation that would take place a few years from now. It's an imaginary conversation, but the sentiment is real.

The two stood on the mountaintop,
The tall mountains made of sand.
The Old Man felt like Moses
As he gazed into The Promised Land.

They were looking west to the sun,
Their backs to the wind and sea,
And the Little Girl, his Joshua, asked,
"How are things going to be?"

"I don't really know," he said.
"I can't tell you what to do,
But remember you're tied to the land
And the land is tied to you.

"What we do with the land God gave us
Might not matter to some,
But I want to save it for you children
And your children yet to come."

Then they walked down to the water's edge
Where ocean meets the sound.
With her hand in his, the Old Man said,
"Just take a look around.

"Not far from here a long time ago, a little girl was born.
Her name was Virginia Dare,
The first girl born in this part of the world,
Least the first to have blond hair.

"When told of her birth all the folk gathered 'round
And sent up a happy cheer,
But soon food ran short, they couldn't go home,
And happiness turned to fear.

"Now, don't know what happened to Virginia Dare,
Your guess is as good as mine.
Those people just melted into the swamps,
A place where the sun don't shine.

"But because they came, others would come
And make a life on these shores.
They'd plant trees and crops,
Open hardware and grocery stores.

"Now, four hundred years later, we've paved miles of road,
Built buildings up to the sky,
But sometimes at night out here by the sea
I can hear Virginia cry.

"She cries for this land and our people,
Land of promise and freedom so dear.
She cries for the woods that are gone now,
For rivers that used to be clear.

"She cries for the farms lost in morning mist,
Replaced with so many malls.
She cries 'cause we've lost so much of our gift,
We can't hear our heart when it calls."

The Old Man finished speaking by the sea that night.
His words took the Little Girl back to the wondrous sight
Of a brave people who came with only a dream.
To be kept alive by the girl in the moonlight's beam.

ABOUT THE AUTHOR

For more than 40 years, Bill Thompson has traveled throughout North Carolina and the South as a speaker for hundreds of organizations from local civic clubs to trade conferences to international conventions. He has been a master of ceremonies and entertainer for hundreds of events celebrating the things that make communities special, from the Hollering Contest in Spivey's Corner and the Wooly Worm Festival in Banner Elk; to the Grits Festival in St. George and Chitlin Strut in Sally, South Carolina; to a "grape stompin'" contest in Tennessee. He's even been a judge at a Sweet Tea Contest in Georgia. In the process, he's had a chance to meet a lot of people and to hear their stories.

As co-host of a local morning television show back in the early 1980s, Bill began to see stories that didn't fit the television format. So he began to write a local newspaper column to tell those stories. Since then, his column has appeared in more than 30 newspapers in North and South Carolina. His column "Front Porch Stories" has been a regular feature in *Our State* magazine, and he has authored two books, *Sweet Tea, Fried Chicken, & Lazy Dogs, A Refection on North Carolina Life*, and *Pearl's Pork Palace and Other Stories from Flynn's Crossing, NC.*

Bill's stories are usually humorous, a reflection of his way of looking at the world around him. Occasionally, he makes a nostalgic odyssey that transports us to a time and place some barely remember and younger folks never had the opportunity to experience. In the process, he not only entertains his audiences, but also helps them appreciate the great traditions and heritage that make North Carolina and the South such a unique aspect of American life.

After many years of association with Boys and Girls Homes of North Carolina, Bill is now retired and spending more time with his family at home in Hallsboro. He continues to write and speak to groups around the country.

If you would like to have Bill speak to your group, call him at (910) 646-4606 or (910) 840-6830, or e-mail at bill.thompson@bghnc.org.